IT'S NOT A
SPRINT

LESSONS OF FAITH AND ENDURANCE ON THE MARATHON OF LIFE

STEPHANIE WALTERS

Ark House Press
arkhousepress.com

Cataloguing in Publication Data:
Title: It's Not A Sprint
ISBN: 978-1-7637720-4-5 (pbk)
Subjects: BIO016000   BIOGRAPHY & AUTOBIOGRAPHY / Sports; REL012170 RELIGION / Christian Living / Personal Memoirs; REL012040 RELIGION / Christian Living / Inspirational

Design by initiateagency.com

ENDORSEMENTS

'Steph's story is an inspiring journey through her early life and young adulthood living with type 1 diabetes — and overcoming hurdle after hurdle. As an exercise physiologist, I often view physical activity as the ultimate life and health enhancer. Steph has shown that it takes a balance of physical fitness, mental health, love, faith, family support, and inspiration. It's impossible to read her memoir and not feel inspired. It goes to show you that life is definitely best approached as a marathon — whether you have diabetes or not.'

Sheri Colberg, PhD
World-leading expert in diabetes and exercise, and author of
'The Athlete's Guide to Diabetes' (and twelve other books)

'Whilst preparing for the Gold Coast Marathon, Steph regularly attended my running group sessions, and I also guided her online. I was impressed by Steph's desire to leave no stone unturned whilst at the same time having to deal with some challenges along the way. Conquering the marathon makes us stronger, and I am thrilled that Steph has taken the time to share her story whilst entwining her newfound strength and love for running.'

Pat Carroll OAM
Former Australian Distance Running Representative

'Steph provides us with an entertaining, highly personal, and inspiring account of her life, set against a backdrop of running, type 1 diabetes, and her ever-present faith. A must-read for anyone seeking motivation to tackle large challenges against the odds.'

Tim Oberg
Founder of Parkrun Australia

'Having had my first interaction with Stephanie over the Internet shortly after I was diagnosed with type 1 diabetes myself, I knew then she was one inspiring woman. Now, reading this beautiful memoir, I cannot help but be thankful our paths crossed. *It's Not a Sprint* is more than a book! It is a beautiful invitation into life, finding and trusting God, and how to experience life despite the challenges it throws at us.

Challenges will come and go in our lives, some stay a little longer than we like, but how amazing it is to have someone like Stephanie who walks the talk (or runs the talk I should say), modelling for us what it looks like to show up for our life and for those around us. As a woman who lives with type 1 diabetes, her resilience and persistence for the things she loves has given me the inspiration and nudge to go live my life doing all the things I love that God has in store for me. I believe regardless of your life circumstances, it will inspire you to do the same too!

This beautiful book, a real and raw share, will be a blessing to anyone who reads it. Let's go live this one amazing God-given life, at our pace. Life is not a sprint! Thank you for writing this life inspiring, life changing book, Stephanie!'

Dr Monica Devanand
Business Growth and Transformation Coach, author, and speaker

'Those who dare to toe the starting line at the Big Red Run are a different breed. Whilst they are all of different abilities and from different backgrounds, the things they have in common are determination, courage, and a desire to explore their physical and mental limits and overcome challenges.

When Stephanie signed up for the 2014 Big Red Run, a fundraising event for the Juvenile Diabetes Research Foundation, she had an additional challenge to face that most others didn't: her type 1 diabetes. Stephanie's spirit and positive attitude were remarkable throughout the six-day run. I recall spending time with her at an aid station when she was suffering from low blood sugars, but there was never any talk of calling it quits. To Stephanie, it was just part of the journey and the challenge.

It's Not a Sprint reflects on not only the challenges endured at the Big Red Run, and the satisfaction of achieving something that seems near impossible, but the highs and lows and many other challenges that Stephanie has taken on, including those that she didn't choose voluntarily.

It's an incredible and adventurous story, and one that will provide hope and inspiration to the many others who live with type 1 diabetes.'

Greg Donovan
Founder of the Big Red Run and Big Red Bash

'*It's Not a Sprint* is an engrossing, engaging story about a young woman's battle with type 1 diabetes, self-confidence, and her role in the world since the age of 5. *It's Not a Sprint* chronicles her journey of faith across literal and figurative deserts to overcome severe hypoglycaemia, recover from a crippling knee injury, survive a heart-wrenching divorce, and embrace the uncertainty of life, the beauty of simply being, and the joy of running from sunrise to sunset and again to sunrise. Stephanie, you had me at "weathered white sandstone walls".'

Don Muchow
Type 1 ultrarunner, and first person to run from Disneyland to Disney World

'Steph's story is one of hope and triumph, proving that through perseverance and a strong unwavering faith, we all have the power within us to keep going and achieve amazing things. It is a story of resilience and strength to challenge the realities of living with type 1 diabetes as an athlete, and to create a life with meaning and purpose through the pursuit of what we love.'

Nicole Bunyon
Founder of Running Mums Australia

FOREWORD

*'There's no way I'm going to let having
type 1 diabetes stand in my way.'*

In ultramarathon running, the most important ingredient for success is the right amount of fuel. Too much food or drink and you feel too heavy and bloated; too little and you don't have enough energy to complete the distance. Your legs feel like tree stumps still attached to the ground, and it takes every ounce of energy to lift them and move forward. You question how far you have to go, and your mind starts to cast doubts whether you can even finish, let alone win a race or get a personal best time.

Now add the extra complication of type 1 diabetes. Your body is continuously crying out for fuel, but it simply can't process that fuel because your pancreas doesn't work, and so you have no insulin to act as the key to let that fuel into your cells. You are starting lightyears behind every other competitor.

Steph discovers through running that if you have faith in yourself and a large degree of stubbornness, if you believe in a higher power that controls your destiny and that all of life's challenges are simply part of a plan, you will find your best self and the person you were always meant to be.

I have run the four corners of this earth from the North Pole to the South and most countries in between. I have run across many countries through snow blizzards, driving rain and searing heat more than once.

I have clocked up close to two hundred thousand kilometres over an ultrarunning career that has spanned more than forty years. I have used running as the tool to save and improve the lives of many thousands of people. I have met with and competed against some of the best distance runners in the world. Yet none of them had to deal with the daily grind of extracting some blood and manually adjusting their glucose levels so that their body wouldn't shut down and leave them lifeless on the side of the road.

In this chronicle, Steph shows that for a person with type one diabetes, every day is a mission. She could easily be excused for simply deciding that mere survival was enough, but instead she excels. Through this book and her deep faith, she unlocks the spirit that we all have and allows us to realise our own potential.

It's Not a Sprint is a manual for life, not just ultrarunning. I am sure you will be inspired, just as I have been after reading about Steph's struggles, to take on the road less travelled and embrace all that it has in store for you.

Pat Farmer AM
Professional ultramarathon runner/adventurer, motivational speaker, and author of *Pole to Pole: One Man, 20 Million Steps*

*'But those who hope in the L*ORD
will renew their strength.
They will soar on wings like eagles;
they will run and not grow weary,
they will walk and not be faint.'
— Isaiah 40:31 (NIV)

'Life is a marathon, not a sprint;
pace yourself accordingly.'
— Amby Burfoot

To God, for giving me the strength to persevere
on the marathon of life, and to Geoff, for
running this wild, wonderful race by my side.

CHAPTER 1

*'That's the beauty of starting lines: Until you begin a
new venture, you never know what awaits you.'*
—Amby Burfoot

BIG RED RUN
DAY 1

2 July 2014

It's still dark as Dad and I walk from our tent towards the Birdsville Hotel.
One thought occupies my mind: *Who in their right mind pays thousands of
dollars for the privilege of running 150 kilometres through a desert?*

I can just make out the Australian flag flying high above the weathered
white sandstone walls and green-trimmed roof. Established in 1884, the
heritage-listed outback pub is on the bucket list of many travellers eager
to boast that they've had a beer at the famous pub. But that could not be
further from my own reason for being here.

It's been nine months since an ad for the Big Red Run popped up in
my Facebook news feed. Greg Donovan founded the event to raise funds
for the Juvenile Diabetes Research Foundation after his son was diagnosed
with type 1 diabetes. This non-profit organisation is dedicated to discover-

ing life-changing breakthroughs to cure, prevent, and treat type 1 diabetes and its complications. As someone living with this condition, this is something I want to get behind.

Set in the heart of the Simpson Desert (renamed in 2019 to Munga-Thirri National Park, meaning *big sandhill country* in the local Aboriginal language), the Big Red Run is Australia's first 250-kilometre multi-day running race. I've signed up for the Little Red Run — the 'easy' option of 150 kilometres — but I'll refer to it as the Big Red Run.

The race consists of two 42.2-kilometre full marathons, two 21.1-kilometre half marathons, and two shorter legs of fifteen and eight kilometres. For an amateur runner like me, the distance I need to cover over the next six days is nothing short of monumental.

The bright red, six-metre-tall inflatable archway leaves me with little doubt where the start line is. *Have I packed everything?* I do my best to reassure myself that I have. I've already packed and repacked my race kit countless times. Still, I do a last-minute check just in case. My backpack is stuffed to the brim; I'm ready for any and every contingency I could possibly face during the Big Red Run.

I have more than enough food for the day, two and a half litres of water, electrolytes, sunscreen, anti-chafing cream, toilet paper, a whistle, compass, fire lighting kit, high visibility vest, head torch, mobile phone with course map installed, hard copy course map, emergency blanket, and first aid kit. Not to mention my insulin and blood glucose meter to manage my type 1 diabetes.

Runners, volunteers, and supporters gather outside the Birdsville Hotel. Volunteers wearing head torches are fitting the runners' bags with GPS tracking devices. Supporters who have travelled thousands of kilometres with their loved ones are chatting happily with one another. Runners are doing last-minute stretches and posing for obligatory pre-race selfies in front of the famous Aussie landmark.

Dad hugs me, and I make my way to the start line.

'Good luck, Steph.'

'Thanks, Dad.' *I'm gonna need it.*

I rummage through my backpack and find my blood glucose meter. I prick my finger with the lancet, drawing a minuscule drop of blood to measure my blood glucose level one last time before the race. Three seconds after applying blood to the test strip, the screen flashes with the number *14.2.*

I'm not surprised to see such a high number (a normal blood glucose reading is between 4.0 and 8.0). The adrenaline coursing through my veins must have caused my blood glucose to spike. I'm not worried because I know it will come down when I start running.

My boyfriend Geoff has written me a note for every day of the race, penned on aged, discoloured paper from a twenty-year-old notebook. Each note is folded in half, its tattered edges sealed with glue. I've placed them in a ziplock bag to protect them from getting damaged by dirt, sweat, and tears.

I take out the first note, and open it to see Geoff's trademark smiley face:

> *Race day 1 — Go Cheekball! Stop thinking about it.*
> *Whatever will be will be. Que sera, sera.*

Since registering for the Big Red Run, I've clocked up hundreds of hours on my feet, running back-to-back long runs on the weekends, trialling my race nutrition, and preparing my mental strategy. And now here I stand on the edge of the Simpson Desert, with nine other Little Red Runners and forty-eight Big Red Runners, as ready as I'll ever be.

But as I wait at the start line amid a sea of orange and blue race shirts, I question myself. Who am I to line up alongside these people who look much fitter, stronger, and more like experienced endurance athletes than I do? A newbie to the sport of ultrarunning, I have no clue what I've gotten myself in for. *Am I a fool to think I can finish this race?*

At seven thirty, the starting gun sends us off on a lap of Birdsville as the sun begins to rise over the town. Birdsville's population of one hundred and fifteen lines the wide, dusty streets to show their support. They must think — know? — we're crazy.

My blood glucose drops before I reach the first checkpoint at the ten-kilometre mark. My hands are trembling when I arrive, making it difficult to prick my finger. Through blurred vision, I make out the number on the screen: *3.2.* I've barely started the race, and I'm already having a hypo!

'I'm sorry, but we can't let you leave until your level is above 6.0,' says Dr Adam, one of the event medics.

'Don't worry about me. I'm fine — really.'

I try to convince Dr Adam that I'm okay as I devour a handful of jelly babies. But he tells me he doesn't have a choice; he has to ground me at the checkpoint until I've eaten enough to bring my blood glucose to a safe level.

Ten minutes later, eager to hit the road, I test my blood glucose again. 3.8. It's still too low. I wait another five minutes and try again. 4.5. *Oh, come on!* One after another, the other runners waltz straight past me through the checkpoint.

After another five minutes, my blood glucose level is 5.2.

'Can I *please* go now?' I beg.

'What else can we get you to eat?' asks Dr Adam. His Pommy accent grates on me, not necessarily because I don't like him but more likely because hypos can make you cranky. I fidget with the straps of my backpack, annoyed that I'm not allowed to leave; I'm not even having a hypo anymore!

I'm relieved to see my blood glucose level reach 6.2. I can finally escape the first checkpoint.

'Are you sure you're feeling ready?' asks Dr Adam. 'You're welcome to hang around here a bit longer if you like.' I understand why he asks this question; hypos can leave you feeling fatigued long after they've been treated.

'No thanks. I'm fine now.'

I'm discouraged that at least half an hour has been wasted, until I remember that Geoff has written me a second note for the first day of the race. I find the ziplock bag buried in the bottom of my backpack, and carefully pull apart the glued ends of the note:

During race day 1 — Marathon!
For serious inspiration — You can dooo it!

Yes, I can! There's no way I'm going to let type 1 diabetes stand in my way.

Despite months of planning for the Big Red Run, I don't have a clue what the Simpson Desert will be like. I expect there'll be plenty of sand, but beyond that, I have no idea what I'll discover here.

To the west of Birdsville lies the longest series of parallel sand dunes in the world, anchored in place by dense vegetation. I need to conquer about twenty dunes today. With my eyes closed, it feels like running on soft sand at the beach. I tackle them one by one, conserving energy with short strides, and stepping on the tracks left by the runners ahead of me.

Running parallel along the crests of the dunes feels surreal. I'm in awe of their untouched beauty, the grains of sand formed into neat ripples by the wind. Splashes of purple and yellow wildflowers dot the landscape, a stark contrast to the dry, cracked earth.

Each climb brings a sense of anticipation as I wonder what awaits me on the other side. At the top of every dune, I'm rewarded with a different yet dramatic vista.

I'm having another hypo when I reach the second checkpoint at twenty-three kilometres. *Poor Dad!* As a volunteer, he must be listening to everything that's happening over his CB radio. My name isn't mentioned due to confidentiality, but Dad would know it's me because the medical team refers to me as 'runner number nine.'

Dad was assigned to the third checkpoint at the thirty-five-kilometre mark, so I'm surprised when I see his Toyota Hilux driving towards me.

'I tried to get information from the medical team, but they weren't giving much away,' he says. The concern in his warm hazel eyes is evident as he watches me munch on trail mix to bring my blood glucose back up.

I'm at this checkpoint even longer than the first. I watch enviously as the other runners pass me. The volunteers cocoon me in an itchy woollen blanket to keep me warm while I wait. They're so lovely, despite how stubborn I am about wanting to leave.

Dr Glenn Singleman, in particular, is incredibly kind and patient. An experienced medical doctor, Glenn is also one of Australia's best-known adventurers and a world record-holding extreme sports athlete. Despite his many impressive accolades, he's one of the most down-to-earth people I've ever met.

My blood glucose level finally rises above 6.0, so I can get moving again — but there's a catch...

'Do you mind running with someone for the rest of the day?' asks Dr Glenn. 'That way, you'll have someone with you in case you have another hypo.'

'Sure, no problem,' I say, anxious to get moving again.

It turns out that my 'running buddy' isn't a runner at all. Meghan uses hiking poles to keep herself steady. Her wild dark curls are tied back in a loose ponytail. She chats away as we dawdle towards the finish line. I enjoy her company greatly and appreciate having someone to share the journey with, but my competitive side doesn't want to come last. I haven't trained for months to walk — I've trained to run!

The final nineteen kilometres stretch on and on. I wear protective cloth coverings called gaiters over my shoes to stop the sand from sneaking in. They don't work all that well, though; I'm forced to sit down after descending into each valley to take off my shoes and pour the granules out. The last thing I want this early in the week is to get blisters from sand rubbing between my toes.

We make it to the final ascent of the day: Nappanerica — famously known as 'Big Red.' While most of the Simpson Desert's dunes are only ten to fifteen metres high, Big Red towers above the rest at forty metres. I hear the persistent *clang, clang, clang* of the race cowbell in the distance; we can't have much further to go. I'm exhausted, but I push on, my shoes disappearing into the sand with each step.

Meghan and I walk together along the crest of Big Red before heading down towards the campsite that's been set up in a valley on a dry lakebed. I welcome the sight of the dark green and olive brown canvas tents, crimson gazebos, blue Portaloos, dusty four-wheel drives and caravans, and orange witch's hats that line our path to the finish line. This will be our 'home' for the next two nights.

After some much-needed recovery food, I nervously make my way to a large whiteboard outside one of the gazebos. The results table for day one is up. My official time is 8:48:31, with an hour of this spent waiting at the checkpoints. I finished in eighth place out of the ten Little Red Runners, and two hours behind the leader Janelle. It isn't exactly the start I'd hoped for.

There's no phone reception in the valley, so Dad and I trudge our way up Big Red to call Mum and Geoff. I groan at the bottom of the dune, sure that every step to the top will hurt, but I know it will be worth it to hear their voices.

My legs feel heavy as I walk back and forth over the top of the dune, the soft sand sliding down either side of the ridge. Finally, my phone displays a single bar of reception, and I touch base with Geoff in Sydney, almost two thousand kilometres away.

'How'd you go, Cheekball?' Geoff asks.

I speak at the speed of light, eager to tell him about my adventurous day in the middle of the desert. I tell him that I'm disappointed about how long it took me to finish the first leg of the race.

'I didn't do as well as I wanted to. If the first day was this tough, I'm worried I won't be able to finish.'

'You're doing awesome. You just ran a marathon! Don't forget, trail running is a lot tougher than road running. You can't expect the same times you're used to. Don't worry about your pace. Just focus on getting to the finish line at the end of day six. I know you can do it.'

I question whether it's possible as I curl up in my sleeping bag that night.

CHAPTER 2

*'Both children and adults like me who live with type 1
diabetes need to be mathematicians, physicians, personal
trainers, and dietitians all rolled into one.'*
—Mary Tyler Moore

11 – 21 June 1993

When I was five years old, I remember being endlessly thirsty and wetting
my pants in the school playground. I remember the GP pricking the tip of
my finger for a drop of blood — the first of over 60,000 finger pricks I've
had in my lifetime. I remember him telling Mum, 'It's very likely that your
daughter has type 1 diabetes. She needs to go straight to hospital.'

I remember sitting in the back seat of our navy-blue Holden Commodore.
I remember the urgency in Mum's voice as she called out to Dad, who was
sitting on the balcony of our second-floor apartment.

'But the Bulldogs are about to start! Are you sure we need to go?' Dad
asked.

I was admitted to Camperdown Children's Hospital in Sydney's inner
west that night. I had a haemoglobin A1c (HbA1C) blood test which shows
your average blood glucose level over the past two or three months. It was
different to the finger prick test I had at the GP's office, which measured
how much glucose I had in my blood at that moment in time. The HbA1C
test confirmed that I had type 1 diabetes.

Contrary to popular belief, type 1 diabetes isn't caused by being overweight or eating too much sugar. It's an incurable autoimmune condition that occurs when your immune system, which normally protects the body against infection, attacks the beta cells in your pancreas that produce insulin.

Insulin is the hormone that helps to move glucose from your bloodstream into the various cells of your body, providing them with the energy they need to function. If too much glucose accumulates in your bloodstream over time, it can become toxic, leading to a myriad of health complications, including heart disease, nerve damage, kidney damage, blindness, and limb amputation.

Blood glucose levels are measured in units called millimoles per litre (mmol/L). The pancreas of a person who doesn't have type 1 diabetes releases the right amount of insulin throughout the day to keep their blood glucose levels between 4.0 and 8.0 mmol/L at all times. Mine was in the high twenties when I was diagnosed!

I spent the next ten days in hospital learning how to do the job of my good-for-nothing pancreas. A nurse taught me how to give myself insulin injections by practising on an orange.

'Your daughter will need at least four injections every day to keep her blood glucose levels within the target range,' she explained to my parents. I don't remember ever fearing needles, but I didn't exactly have a choice. Either I accepted that I needed to do this to stay alive, or I let my body slowly starve itself.

Although I learned early on how to inject myself, I relied on Mum and Dad to draw up the right amount of insulin before each meal. I didn't learn to do this myself until I was in high school, so Dad volunteered as a 'parent helper' on my grade six camp in Canberra. As well as looking after me, he helped the teachers round up the kids at tourist attractions like Questacon and Parliament House.

I also had to prick my fingers up to eight times each day to monitor my blood glucose levels. Initially I'd wince as the tiny needle pierced through my soft skin, but over the years my fingers have become hard and calloused, so it rarely hurts now.

I learned that if I was below 4.0 (called hypoglycaemia, or 'hypo' for short), I could experience symptoms such as excess sweating, fatigue, hunger, fainting, irritability, shakiness, blurred vision, and slurred speech. I'd need to eat fifteen grams of carbohydrates to bring my blood glucose back up to a safe range.

If I was above 8.0 (called hyperglycaemia), the symptoms could include increased thirst, headaches, trouble concentrating, blurred vision, frequent urination, and fatigue. I'd have to take an extra dose of insulin to bring my blood glucose back down.

I wish the treatment for type 1 diabetes was as simple as it sounds, but there are a million and one things that can affect blood glucose levels. Even if you eat the *exact* same foods and inject the *exact* same amount of insulin, your blood glucose levels can be *completely different* from one day to the next. Other factors that can affect them include exercise, stress, illness, dehydration, medication, sleep, hormones, and temperature, to name just a handful. It's complex, and you'll never achieve perfection, no matter how hard you try.

The exact cause of type 1 diabetes is unknown, however genetics and environmental factors may both play a role in increasing a person's risk of developing it. For decades, researchers have been searching for triggers, such as viral infections and certain toxins in the air or foods. I'd been sick with a virus not long before I was diagnosed, so the doctors concluded that this was what triggered the condition in me.

When my identical twin sister Melissa visited me in the hospital, the doctors recommended that she should have an HbA1C blood test too. When one identical twin has type 1 diabetes, the other has a one in three chance of developing it. Mum and Dad awaited the results with trepidation, but thankfully the test came back negative.

My hospital stay was the first time I'd ever been separated from Melissa, and I missed her terribly. I remember looking into a full-length mirror and being convinced that she was staring back at me. I burst into tears when I realised it was my own reflection.

Melissa and I have always shared a special bond that someone who doesn't have a twin wouldn't get. How can you *not* be best friends with someone you shared a womb with? As identical twins, we have one hundred per cent identical DNA so we're as close as two people can possibly be.

We're quite unique when it comes to being twins because we don't share a birthday. Mum gave birth to Melissa via a vaginal delivery twenty-five minutes *before* midnight, whereas I was born by emergency caesarean twenty-five minutes *after* midnight. I guess it was cosy in there and I didn't want to budge!

Although it's easy to tell us apart now, that wasn't always the case. Strangers used to greet me on the street, mistaking me for Melissa. I'm sure they thought I was rude when I stared blankly back at them. Even I struggle to work out who is who in our baby photos! We also had our own secret language as toddlers, and would play pranks on people over the phone as teenagers because our voices sound so similar.

One night in hospital, the staff brought me a giant bowl of peas for dinner. Nothing else. Seriously, who would think that a five-year-old would want to eat that? Even as a child I didn't like to cause a fuss and would stay quiet even if I was deeply unhappy. But my parents complained until the staff eventually gave me a bowl of vanilla ice cream instead — a small victory in a world suddenly fraught with uncertainty.

As we left the safety of the hospital, my parents couldn't have predicted how all-encompassing the impact of my diagnosis would be. There was the constant worry about what could happen if they accidentally gave me too much insulin. The fear that I might have a hypo overnight and not wake up the next morning. The need for vigilance to make sure my insulin doses were just right for my carbohydrate intake. The desire to provide me with a 'normal' childhood, yet having to poke me multiple times a day with needles.

I'm sure my parents took the diagnosis much harder than I did — I was too young to fully understand what it meant. They felt a sense of guilt over something they believed was their fault, even though they didn't do anything to give me type 1 diabetes. They would have done anything to take it from me, but they couldn't. I can only imagine how difficult that burden was to bear.

1998

When I was a kid, I'd often lie to Mum and Dad about my blood glucose levels because I didn't want them to worry about me. If I did a finger prick and saw that I was having a hypo, I'd hurry to turn my blood glucose meter off before they caught a glimpse of the number on the screen, tell them my level was four point something, and sneak a handful of jellybeans.

At the age of ten, I was lying on our vibrant yellow couch, indulging in nineties cartoon classics such as *Captain Planet* and *Hey Arnold!*, when I had a severe hypo that caused me to lose consciousness. In a situation like this, when someone is unable to consume carbohydrates by mouth, an emergency medicine called glucagon must be injected.

Glucagon is a hormone that triggers the liver to release stored glucose into the bloodstream.

Mum and Dad were too scared to give me the injection in case they did it incorrectly, so they immediately called triple zero. It must have been terrifying for them to be so close to losing their child; I don't know how I would have reacted in a situation like theirs.

By the time the ambulance arrived, I was so disorientated that I couldn't even tell the paramedics my name or what day of the week it was! Thankfully, within ten minutes of being injected with glucagon, my blood glucose levels were within normal range again.

This wouldn't be the last time I'd find myself on the brink of life and death.

CHAPTER 3

'I believe in Christianity as I believe that the sun has risen, not only because I see it but because by it, I see everything else.'
—C.S. Lewis

1999 – 2005

I haven't always loved running. My first memory of running was at my primary school athletics carnival in grade six. I showed up on the morning and decided it would be a good idea to enter the hundred-metre sprint. I hadn't trained for it, but I figured it would be the easiest event because the distance was the shortest.

The race wasn't run on a proper athletics track. Instead, it unfolded on the same worn-out grass field where every other school sport was played. It was the same spot where all the students had to congregate on the many occasions that the school had a fire scare or bomb threat (usually a prank by a kid who didn't want to go to class that day).

I wish I could tell you that I finished in first place and my passion for running kickstarted that day. But I'm sorry to say I came dead last. That was my first and last competitive hundred-metre race! I don't remember feeling embarrassed or anything. But at that moment I formed the belief that I'd always be a slow runner, and that sprinting just wasn't my cup of tea.

I was fairly good at cross-country running though. I'd turn up on the day and just run. Oh, to have the energy I had as a kid again! I made it into my high school's zone cross-country team two years in a row. These were the highlights of my otherwise mediocre school sporting career since I sucked at every other form of physical activity.

The zone events were held at Hurlstone Agricultural College in Glenfield in Sydney's south-west. My standout memory was tramping through cow dung that had been camouflaged by the muddy brown trails. Needless to say, my love of running didn't begin with cross-country either.

It also didn't begin in grade twelve, when Melissa, our best friend Aurelle, and I decided we should go for runs together. Aurelle lived just across the road from our house in Wattle Grove in Sydney's south-west. Although she went to a different high school, we did homework together after school every afternoon. We had many Friday night sleepovers and disco parties, bonding over our love of the Spice Girls, *Harry Potter*, and Mexican food.

We were already going on regular walks around the block with our Cavalier King Charles Spaniel, Lucy, and Aurelle's Beagle, Rocky. We'd drop into our local Coles supermarket to pick up our favourite lollies, usually Nerds, and then stop by the nearby basketball courts so that Melissa could check out a boy she had a crush on while pretending to be interested in playing basketball.

I'm afraid our running phase was short-lived. In fact, Aurelle recently admitted to me, 'There were times I didn't want you to knock on my door!'

November 2005 – April 2006

In November 2005, fresh from completing the final exams for our Higher School Certificate, Melissa and I celebrated turning eighteen. Sitting at the well-loved wooden table in my parents' backyard, we had a lively discussion with our friends about religion.

Melissa and I were christened in a Greek Orthodox church as babies, but I only remember going to church for events like weddings and christenings. So I grew up knowing very little about Christianity (or any religion for that matter). I never doubted that God existed. If someone asked me, I'd tell them I was a Christian, but I didn't understand what it truly meant to be one.

I didn't recognise that I was rebelling against God, and I certainly didn't think I needed his forgiveness. After all, what had I ever done wrong? I was a good person, right? Sure, I'd tell 'white lies' to get out of trouble, or disobey Mum and Dad when I thought they were being unfair. But it's not as if I'd murdered anyone!

At the age of fifteen, Melissa and I attended a Roman Catholic church with Aurelle. I thought it was a 'good' thing to go to church — that I could work my way into Heaven. I learned a little bit about Jesus, but I wasn't living with Him as my King. I lived my life in much the same way as I had previously, ignoring the One who'd given me life.

At my eighteenth birthday party, I learned that one of my friends was a Mormon. I must have shown interest in what she shared because the next day she brought over a copy of the Book of Mormon. I read it from cover to cover, and found myself walking into her church on a Sunday morning in early December. Not knowing much about Jesus, I believed what the Church of Jesus Christ of Latter-day Saints (more commonly known as Mormonism) taught about Him.

In January 2006, I enrolled to study a Bachelor of Nutrition and Dietetics at Charles Sturt University. I moved five hours from Sydney to Wagga Wagga, a major regional city in the Riverina region of New South Wales, in hopes of one day becoming a qualified dietitian to help others living with type 1 diabetes. (Looking back, this makes no rational sense to me because I've always had an aversion to visiting dietitians!)

I quickly joined the Mormon church there. I also joined an evangelical, or Bible-believing, Christian church on campus. I remember thinking to myself, *Mormons believe in Jesus, so I must be a Christian!* I became frustrated when my Christian friends told me that there's a lot of false teaching within Mormonism. As my husband will tell you, I can be quite stubborn; I didn't want to admit that what they were saying might be true.

In April 2006, I became the first person to be baptised in a new Mormon temple that had just been built in Wagga Wagga. I was dressed all in white; I had to make sure my outfit remained opaque when it got wet! But even as I was fully submerged in water, all I could think was, *Am I making a mistake? What if my friends are right?* I was starting to seriously question my beliefs.

A week later, I was sitting in the front row at the evangelical church when I was challenged by a sermon on Galatians 1:6-8, where Paul says, 'I am astonished that you are so quickly deserting him who called you in the grace of Christ and are turning to a different gospel — not that there is another one, but there are some who trouble you and want to distort the gospel of Christ. But even if we or an angel from heaven should preach to you a gospel contrary to the one we preached to you, let him be accursed.'

This is exactly what Mormonism teaches — that an angel named Moroni visited a young American man named Joseph Smith in 1823, and gave him a new 'gospel' (the Greek word meaning *good news*) called the Book of Mormon.

Over the next few weeks, I investigated the differences between Christianity and Mormonism late into the night in my cramped room on the university campus. I didn't care about my looming assignment deadlines; this was so much more important.

I began studying the Bible for myself, especially the claims that Jesus made about Himself. A verse that stood out to me was John 14:6, where Jesus says, 'I am the way and the truth and the life. No one comes to the Father except through me.' I had real doubts that the Jesus of Mormonism was the Jesus I should be following.

One evening in the Charles Sturt University Library, my Christian friend Scott encouraged me to think about why I believed what I did. He was super clued in on the inconsistencies within Mormon teaching. He showed me that unlike the Book of Mormon, the Bible stands up against scrutiny as a reliable and infallible document. It's possible to demonstrate this by checking it against the thousands of detailed prophecies it has accurately predicted, the historical accounts it records, as well as the scientific facts it confirms.

I also discovered that Christians and Mormons have opposing views on what we need to do to get into Heaven. Ephesians 2:8-9 says, 'For by grace you have been saved through faith. And this is not your own doing; it is the gift of God, not a result of works, so that no one may boast.'

Grace is God's unmerited favour towards those who don't deserve it. Mormons believe that we can't be saved by grace alone, but that we must also do good works. They strive for perfection by trying to obey the Ten Commandments, falsely believing that both faith and works are necessary for salvation.

The Bible, on the other hand, teaches that *no one* is good enough to earn their own way into Heaven. Romans 3:23 says, 'For all have sinned and fall short of the glory of God', and Romans 6:23 says, 'For the wages of sin is death, but the free gift of God is eternal life in Christ Jesus our Lord.'

That same night, I renounced the false teaching of Mormonism, and signed up to run the race of faith in the true Jesus of the Bible. I prayed, *Lord, I'm so sorry for failing to live with You as my King. I'm sorry for thinking that I could work my own way into Heaven, instead of trusting in Jesus alone for my salvation.*

I now understood what it meant to be a Christian. I understood that God loves us so much that He sent His only Son Jesus into the world, to take the punishment that we rightly deserve for rebelling against Him. He holds out the gift of eternal life in His hands, if only we'd grasp it in our own. And we can do this not by relying on the 'good' stuff that we do, but by trusting in Jesus' death and resurrection. That truly is good news!

CHAPTER 4

'Good philosophy must exist, if for no other reason,
because bad philosophy needs to be answered.'
—C.S. Lewis

May 2006

Shortly after making the life-changing decision to follow Jesus, I had a revelation that the pursuit of career and financial success would never bring me lasting joy. My purpose in life had become to glorify God and enjoy Him forever.

So I switched from studying Nutrition and Dietetics to a Bachelor of Arts, with a major in Philosophy and minors in English Literature and Sociology. I loved every second of it! I wasn't naive; I knew it was unlikely that I'd end up with a career in the field. But I knew in my heart that I was following God's calling for my life.

As a Philosophy student, I had the opportunity to explore life's biggest questions:

> *What is the meaning of life?*
> *Where did we come from?*
> *Is there a God?*
> *Is there life after death?*

Why is there suffering in the world?
Is there absolute right and wrong?

I went on to complete my Honours degree in Philosophy under the supervision of Dr Graeme McLean. A graduate of the University of Oxford, Graeme is easily the most brilliant man I have ever met. But he isn't just a scholar; he's a gentleman.

Graeme became my Christian mentor and role model as I took my first steps as a new believer. He taught me how important it is to 'Always be prepared to give an answer to everyone who asks you to give the reason for the hope that you have' (1 Peter 3:15, NIV). And for that I will be eternally grateful.

🏃 🏃 🏃

June – December 2006

A clumsy moment during a friendly tennis match led to disaster. Scott hit an impressive lob over my head that landed at the baseline. Keeping my eye on the ball, I ran backwards, only to trip over my own feet. The patella in my right knee dislocated, and I fell on my butt.

Not wanting to look like a sook in front of three guys, I got straight back up — at least I tried to. There was a disturbing *crunch* as my knee buckled beneath me. I couldn't place any weight on it without experiencing excruciating pain, so my friends called for an ambulance.

Mum and Dad had already invested so much money for me to live and study on campus; the last thing I wanted them to have to worry about was an ambulance bill. But none of my friends owned cars, and this was long before ride-sharing apps came onto the scene.

After that day, I suffered recurrent patella dislocations. My knee would often give way when I stepped on an uneven surface. Although the pain usually didn't last long, it was enough to impact my confidence when running. It slowed me down because of the fear that it might happen again if I accidentally stepped in a hole or tripped over a rock.

One afternoon in early December, I set out on a bike ride. I turned a corner and noticed a ute speeding towards me. I panicked, and quickly spun the handlebars to avoid it. I lost control of the bike as the tyres skidded across the road. I fell off, landing awkwardly, and heard a *pop* as my knee dislocated. My knee was on fire! The driver didn't stop to check if I was okay, leaving me lying there in agony.

Thankfully, I wasn't too far from home and was able to hobble my way back. But I was still limping days later, spending hours on the couch with a bag of peas wrapped around my knee. Mum drove the five hours from Sydney to Wagga Wagga to take care of me while I completed the final semester of my first year of university.

When I was back home in Sydney for the holidays, Mum took me to a top orthopaedic surgeon in Liverpool. He told me that my best option was to have a knee arthroscopy, a routine surgical procedure that can diagnose and treat problems in the knee joint. He'd make a couple of small incisions, insert a tiny camera into my knee, and use instruments to correct any issues. So I had the surgery in mid-December, followed by four months of physiotherapy.

10 August 2007

I was standing in the foyer of the Charles Sturt University Library when Mum called me with the news: 'Please don't worry, but Mel's in hospital.' I could tell she was trying hard to keep her voice steady.

At the age of nineteen, Melissa had been diagnosed with type 1 diabetes — fourteen years after my own diagnosis. She'd been ill with glandular fever in the lead up to her diagnosis, and her doctor believed this was the trigger for her to develop the condition.

Because I was diagnosed as a child, I have no memory of a life without type 1 diabetes. But perhaps this was a blessing. For one thing, I would have had more junk food and sugary soft drinks during my childhood, without a care for how they might affect my health. But for Melissa, who had never needed to worry about counting carbs and taking injections, I can only imagine how challenging it must have been to come to terms with the diagnosis.

My heart broke for my twin sister. A sense of helplessness I'd never experienced before weighed me down. I was desperate to get home to give her a hug and reassure her that everything would be okay. I boarded the six-hour CountryLink train home the following morning.

🏃 🏃 🏃

9 August 2009

I wouldn't blame you if you assumed that the knee surgery put me off ever running again. But almost two years later, and a decade after losing miserably in the hundred-metre sprint, I entered another running race. Mum somehow convinced me to run the City2Surf with her.

The City2Surf is the world's largest fun run, covering fourteen kilometres between Hyde Park in Sydney's central business district and the world-famous Bondi Beach in the eastern suburbs. Mum had run the previous year's City2Surf, and has since completed another sixteen, with a goal to complete twenty in a row (although I guarantee she'll surpass that number). Over the years, she has used the race to raise thousands of dollars for the Juvenile Diabetes Research Foundation.

I had no clue what I was getting myself in for as I stood at the start line with Mum and 80,000 others. I was overweight, out of shape, and unhappy. I thought that using the term 'fun run' to describe fourteen kilometres of pure torture was an oxymoron.

When Mum left me at the infamous 'Heartbreak Hill', a steep two-kilometre ascent from Rose Bay to Vaucluse along New South Head Road, I thought I was going to die. But I didn't; I crossed the finish line in 1:52:01 — almost six minutes behind Mum!

As I dipped my blistered feet into the ocean, soaking in the post-race atmosphere, I had a light-bulb moment. I began to understand why three million Australians participate in the sport of running. I was experiencing what's called the 'runner's high' — a feeling of euphoria coupled with reduced anxiety and pain that runners sometimes get during and after intense exercise. Studies show that the runner's high is caused by the natural release of feel-good chemicals called endorphins and endocannabinoids.

I wanted more of that. But life got in the way, and I didn't experience that incredible feeling again until 2011.

One of the highlights of the City2Surf for me is the musical entertainment spread across the entire fourteen kilometres — the pop tunes played by locals enjoying the race from the comfort of their balconies; the beating drums and guitar strums of rock bands performing from rooftops; the Nova 96.9 radio team set up with gigantic speakers, blasting what my parents would call 'doof-doof music'.

It must be my fourteen per cent Scottish genetic composition, but my favourite is the kilt-clad bagpipe players, whose soul-stirring melodies give me the strength to keep running. Their beautiful ballads force my mind to drift back to the rugged highlands of Scotland...

CHAPTER 5

'It is not the mountain we conquer, but ourselves.'
—Sir Edmund Hillary

October 2009

In late 2009, I had a once-in-a-lifetime opportunity to spend three and a half months in Europe. I'd won a scholarship for a Philosophy exchange program at Lancaster University in north-west England! I spent eight nights of the mid-term 'study break' exploring the wilderness of Scotland on a shoestring budget.

I stayed the first three nights in Oban, a relatively busy seaside town on the west coast of Scotland. Tourists often choose Oban as a base from which to explore the surrounding islands.

My first day didn't quite go to plan. The relentless rain dampened my spirits, and at one point I veered off course. I was alone in a strange place, and struggled to decipher the robust Scottish accent. There's only so many times you can ask someone to repeat themselves before you should nod your head, say 'thanks', and move on.

But suddenly the most spectacular rainbow appeared. Its gentle bands of colour stretched across the sky, blending from soft golden hues to deep berry tones, with cool greens and blues shimmering in between. It reminded me that even when life doesn't quite go to plan, God is always looking out for me. I reflected upon the abundance of beauty in the world, and the creativity of God who so generously shares it with us.

I resolved not to let the weather ruin my day. I walked up the steep hill to a Colosseum-looking structure called McCaig's Tower. The sun's rays glimmered through the archways, and bare trees and fallen autumn leaves lined the path to the top. I looked out over Oban Bay, with its characteristic brown and white houses crowned by pointed roofs, and fishing boats bobbing in the water.

My next stop was the Isle of Mull. As the ferry approached the island, I pulled out my phone and snapped a photo of Duart Castle, a lonely little castle perched on black volcanic rock. I also saw snow dusting the peak of a mountain in the distance. I couldn't believe it at first because I'd never seen snow before!

When I arrived at Craignure, a small village on the Isle of Mull, I didn't have a clue what I should do for the rest of the afternoon. Duart Castle closes for the winter, so I couldn't see it up-close.

'I only have three hours to spend on the island,' I told the snowy-haired man at the tourist information centre. 'What should I see?'

'Och! Ye mist catch a bus tae Tobermory!' he said.

Tobermory is the largest populated city on the island — which isn't saying much. It's a quaint harbour town, famous for its fish and chips, as well as the row of brightly coloured houses by the glistening water. I stocked up on food supplies from an old church building that had been converted into a Spar supermarket.

My journey took me to the Isle of Iona, a small island measuring just six kilometres long by two kilometres wide. I had to take a bus and two ferries to reach the remote island. I didn't pick the best day to arrive; it was windy and drizzling. But my mood lifted when I spotted a couple of Highland cows. They were so adorable with their long horns and thick shaggy coats.

The Isle of Iona is most famous for Iona Abbey, a Celtic Christian monastery established by Saint Columba in AD 563. From here, Christianity spread throughout the rest of Scotland, and the abbey remains a place of pilgrimage for many Christians. It wasn't difficult to see why as I roamed its crumbling, history-laden ruins.

I stayed in a simple, secluded hostel on a picturesque beach, with an outlook towards the Treshnish Isles, an archipelago formed by numerous uninhabited islands. I was the only soul staying in the hostel — even the receptionist disappeared right after I checked in! The window in my room didn't shut completely, no matter how hard I tried to budge it. I barely slept that night as I shivered against the chill drifting in from the North Atlantic Ocean.

The next day, I hopped on a train from Oban to Fort William (often described as the 'Outdoor Capital of the United Kingdom'), before catching a taxi to my hostel in Glen Nevis. I caught up on some much-needed sleep and felt relaxed when I woke up the following morning.

I decided I'd attempt to climb Ben Nevis, the tallest mountain in the United Kingdom at 1,345 metres above sea level. I wasn't ready to call myself a 'runner' at this stage, but I did enjoy hiking. I thrive on challenges that drive me to push past boundaries I never thought possible, and Ben Nevis would be the perfect location to test both my physical and mental limits.

I knew to expect snow because I could see it on the top of the mountain from its base. The weather forecast hinted at clear skies, although there would be 'blustery' conditions close to the summit. I didn't know what that word meant, but Google gave me a definition: '(of weather) characterised by strong winds.'

The *Visit Scotland* website warned me that 'climbing Ben Nevis in the winter is only for experienced mountaineers.' I also read that people had lost their lives on its slopes due to avalanches. The name 'Ben Nevis' itself can be translated from the ancient Gaelic language as either *mountain with its head in the clouds*, or *venomous mountain* — I preferred the sound of the former!

Still, I figured I might as well give it a go. When would I get this chance again? If I found it unsafe to continue, I'd turn back. I was by no means an 'experienced mountaineer', and I knew not to take any risks if it wasn't safe to do so.

As the trek began, I marvelled at the scenery — the oak trees dotted with golden orange autumn leaves, the moss-covered granite rocks lining the path, and the sweeping blue waterfalls.

Little did I know that I'd soon be battling through a blizzard, with snow halfway up to my knees! I was nowhere near prepared for the conditions. Although I had a decent waterproof jacket, I wore thin tracksuit pants, and my hiking boots were pretty average.

A friendly-looking group of hikers approached me while I was taking a snack break that consisted of a Scottish soft drink called Iron Bru and a mini-Mars Bar (not exactly the nutrition of an 'experienced mountaineer').

'Hullo! How urr ye daein'?' said a tall, red-haired Scotsman with a broad smile.

'Oh, g'day! I'm okay. Just trying to decide if I should keep going or turn back here.'

'Ah, ye'r Australian? Stick wi' us 'n' we'll hulp ye up th' ben!'

I translated his words to mean I could walk with the group, so I followed behind them. I'm so glad I did because they clearly knew what they were doing!

Philippians 4:13 echoed through my mind, especially in the last hour when my calves were screaming: 'I can do all things through Christ who strengthens me' (NKJV). And with God's help, I finally made it to the summit of Ben Nevis! The snow-covered ruins of an old weather observatory stood striking against the white mist hovering over the peak.

I didn't stick around on the summit for as long as I would have liked. My gloves did little to protect my hands from the cold, so I was worried about the real possibility of frost bite. I also had poor visibility due to the thick fog, and gale force winds turned my cheeks red. I made it back to the hostel eight or so hours after my hike had begun, my legs wobbly like jelly.

My final destination was Glencoe, but not before a six-hour detour via Mallaig. I was eager to cross Glenfinnan Viaduct, the bridge that Harry and Ron flew over in their blue Ford Anglia in the film *Harry Potter and the Chamber of Secrets*. Scotland's West Highland Line, which travels through a rugged landscape of mountains, lochs, and countryside, is among the most famous railway journeys in the world.

When I reached Glencoe, my hamstrings were still aching from my climb up Ben Nevis; I don't think the long train journey would have helped. So I thought it'd be a good idea to take a gentle stroll the following day.

There were many places I wanted to see in Glencoe, but none more so than the Lost Valley (or 'Coire Gabhail' in Gaelic), a hidden valley steeped in both history and mystery. It was here that the Macdonalds, the oldest and largest of all Scottish clans, hid cattle they'd allegedly stolen from the Campbell clan. It was also where a tragic massacre took place in 1692, when Campbell soldiers killed thirty-eight members of the Macdonald clan.

I'd printed out a guide telling me the walk would take two to three hours. *Easy*, I thought to myself. I wasn't aware, however, that the beginning of the track was over an hour's walk from the hostel! But I couldn't complain when I reached a panorama that opened out to deep valleys, towering mountains, and dense greenery as far as the eye could see.

I eventually made it to the Three Sisters, the name given to the three ridges of a mountain called Bidean nam Bian. The giant rock formations that had been carved out by glaciers and volcanic explosions centuries ago were nothing short of majestic. In fact, Glencoe's awe-inspiring landscape has become the backdrop for major film and television productions, including one of my favourites, *Braveheart*.

Multiple tracks wind their way up to Bidean nam Bian. I took the one I believed led to the Lost Valley, but I got lost looking for it! I was meant to walk along the track between the two sisters on the *left*, which would have been a four-kilometre return journey. Instead, I took the track between the two sisters on the *right*, resulting in a disconcerting river crossing via slippery stepping stones, as well as a scramble along a narrow trail beside a steep cliff.

A light drizzle of rain began shortly after I realised I'd gone the wrong way. I slid down a precarious section of the trail on my butt, before having to walk all the way back to the start of the track, and then back up the correct one. My spirits lifted at the sight of a herd of red deer roaming gracefully over the rocky terrain.

As I stepped into the serenity of the Lost Valley, towering rock walls loomed overhead, their rugged peaks shrouded in mist. A crisp breeze brushed against my skin, carrying the earthy scent of damp moss and the distant sound of a trickling stream.

I was confident that I'd never again set foot in a more beautiful part of the world. I couldn't help but wonder, though: *How did the Macdonalds get their cattle up here in the first place?*

CHAPTER 6

*'Running is kind of like coffee. The first time you drink it you
might not like it. It's bitter and leaves a bad taste in your mouth,
but you kind of like the way it makes you feel. However, after
a few times, it starts to taste better and then all of a sudden
you're hooked and it's the new best part of waking up.'*
—Amy Hastings

1 January 2011 – 16 September 2012

My love of running was ignited at the Ernie Smith Reserve hockey fields
in Moorebank in Sydney's south-west. I was barely able to run fifty metres.
My lungs searched frantically for oxygen as I ran each lap, and it took great
strength to lift my feet off the ground. But I knew my life had changed forever.

My then-husband and I decided it was time to get in shape as one of our
New Year's resolutions. We'd both put on a substantial amount of weight
since our wedding in September 2008. We'd miraculously survived on a diet
of Cadbury chocolate, Kentucky Fried Chicken and Pepsi Max, and had no
cardiovascular fitness or muscle tone to speak of. Something had to give…

I also had poor control of my type 1 diabetes. Every three months, I
had appointments with an endocrinologist — a doctor who specialises in
glands and the hormones they produce (in my case, the pancreas and insulin). Before each visit, I'd fill in my little logbook with imaginary blood glu-

cose levels, wanting to avoid the raised eyebrows and disappointed glances I knew would come if I didn't. I made sure I didn't only write down perfect levels, but sprinkled in the odd *3.6* and *15.8* so he wouldn't suspect I was making them up.

Like many people with type 1 diabetes, I used my condition as an excuse *not* to exercise, saying I was too scared I'd have a hypo. I hated PE at high school. I was worried that I'd embarrass myself if my blood glucose levels dropped too low during class. I'd learned from experience that I could have hypos even up to two days *after* exercise, depending on the type of exercise and how strenuous it was.

But eventually I came to a point where I acknowledged that I needed to quit using my useless pancreas as an excuse! So I picked up a copy of *The Diabetic Athlete* by Dr Sheri Colberg, an exercise physiologist who has lived well with type 1 diabetes since 1968. I gained so much knowledge and practical tools to help me safely manage the risk of hypos during and after exercise.

Having type 1 diabetes means I need to spend time meticulously planning my exercise. I need to think about what I can do to avoid a hypo, as well as what to do if I do have one. I need to be smart about what foods I eat and when. I need to monitor my blood glucose levels before, during, and after exercise.

I learned that there's no one-size-fits-all approach for every person with type 1 diabetes. Through trial and error, I found that eating my last meal at least two hours before a run helped me avoid mid-run hypos. And what works for one type of exercise won't work for another. A one-hour, low intensity run can cause my blood glucose to drop, while fifteen minutes of high intensity sprints can cause it to spike.

With the right knowledge and strategies in place, being a runner with type 1 diabetes is not just possible — it's very much achievable!

I would run around the hockey fields after the sun had gone down. I preferred running at night; I didn't want to run where people could see every part of my body jiggling. I even bought a fancy treadmill so I could run at home when my then-husband was working night shifts.

The only thing I like about treadmills is the convenience factor; I'd much rather run in the fresh air outdoors. Nothing slows down time like being on a treadmill for half an hour, only to look at the screen and realise you've only clocked up three minutes. I soon realised that no one actually gives a stuff what I look like when I'm running, and I gained enough confidence to venture outdoors.

In August 2011, I ran my second City2Surf, finishing in 1:33:07 and beating my 2009 time by thirteen minutes. I knew that I could never again use my type 1 diabetes as an excuse not to exercise. In fact, I'd be crazy to *not* exercise! It improves overall blood glucose management, helps maintain a healthy body weight, increases energy levels, lowers blood pressure, reduces the likelihood of developing heart disease, and decreases the symptoms of both depression and anxiety.

I'd well and truly caught the running bug by 2012. I ran not one, not two, but four races! This included my third City2Surf in August (which I ran in 1:24:27, breaking my personal best time by over eight minutes), followed by the half marathon at the Sydney Running Festival in September. That's right — I ran 21.1 kilometres! I felt like I'd finally earned the title of 'runner'.

November 2012

I might not be here today if it wasn't for my dog Chelsea.

My then-husband and I had been fighting. I don't remember what the argument was about; I only remember him leaving the house to go out drinking with his friends, and me going to bed in tears. I must have already been having a hypo by that stage. I'd injected insulin for dinner but was too upset to eat, so this would have sent my blood glucose levels even lower.

I don't know how many hours passed before Chelsea woke me up. She was standing over me with her tiny front paws on my chest, frantically licking my face and whining. Chelsea's exact breed is a mystery. A vet once told me that she looked like a Pomeranian crossed with an Australian Terrier, so she's only a little thing, and would have been trying her hardest to wake me up.

It took me a while to comprehend what was happening. I was drenched in sweat, dazed, and barely able to move. Thankfully, there was a packet of lollies on the bedside table next to me. I gobbled down a handful until I began to feel normal again.

Any person with type 1 diabetes who has experienced a hypo like this knows how frightening it can be. Many don't wake up like I did. I was flooded with emotion when the reality of what Chelsea had done hit me. After saving her life from an animal shelter the previous year, my four-legged friend had returned the favour.

CHAPTER 7

'To be a Christian means to forgive the inexcusable
because God has forgiven the inexcusable in you.'
—C.S. Lewis

21 – 25 December 2012

I discovered that my ex-husband was cheating on me the very same day I prayed to God asking for a sign one way or another.

I'd had my suspicions for a year or so. He'd become increasingly withdrawn and was rarely home. When he *was* home, he'd spend hours playing video games, immersed in a world of his own with no room for me in it. I wondered what he was trying to escape from. Problems at work? Our relationship?

He'd been screening phone calls from unknown numbers, and a worried look etched over his face every time his phone rang. He also refused to tell me the pin number to unlock his phone, even when he was driving and needed me to open Google Maps for directions.

I was in bed one night when he came home with the smell of beer on his breath. He stared silently at me for the longest time.

'What's wrong, sweetie?' I asked.

He didn't say anything for a while. He just kept staring at me. It was like he wanted to tell me something, but he didn't know how because he knew it would hurt me. Finally, he said, 'I'm sorry I'm not the husband I should be for you, Steph.'

I didn't know what he meant, but I was too afraid to ask.

A few days before Christmas Day 2012, I secretly watched over his shoulder as he entered the pin number into his phone. The next day, as he took a nap to recover from Man Flu, I carefully pulled his phone out from under his pillow and retreated to the bathroom. We were living in a shoe box at the time and there was nowhere else I could go.

I read his text messages. I found out he'd been lying to me about working out at the gym when he'd in fact been out drinking with his friends. I scrolled through his call log. There were numbers I didn't recognise, but I rationalised that they could be work-related.

I clicked into his email account. One after another, I read conversations he'd had with countless women I didn't know via a classified advertisements website called Craigslist.

I sat on the toilet silently bawling my eyes out. In one ad, he wrote, *I'm married but that's nearly over.* Interesting — he never mentioned that to me. Another ad said, *Just broke up with long time partner. Looking for a bit of fun at my place.* While I was away on a women's church camp, he'd possibly been sleeping with someone in our bed. Every message felt like a dagger to the heart, with each piercing deeper than the one before.

Nothing I read surprised me, perhaps because I'd suspected it for so long. I took screenshots of the conversations and sent them to my own phone. He was still fast asleep when I returned to the bedroom. I didn't want to confront him while he was sick.

Besides, my emotions were running wild, and I couldn't guarantee I wouldn't say something I'd later regret. But I knew I had to face the music sooner or later. My first love and high school sweetheart, the man I'd shared eight years of my life with, had betrayed me.

I plucked up the courage to talk to him the next day. 'I know you've been cheating on me.' He denied it at first — until I showed him the screenshots.

'I love you, Steph. Please don't leave me,' he begged. But he didn't say the one word I wanted to hear: *Sorry*. Instead, he tried to justify what he'd done.

'I never actually met any of them.' I didn't believe him.

'I need space. I need time to process all of this,' I said.

We separated on Christmas Eve. Not wanting to ruin Christmas for our families, we didn't let them know what was going on. We let everyone believe that everything was okay. I did a hopeless job of it. I had to sit next to him, pretending that this Christmas was no different from any other — that we were happy. I lost count of the number of times I found myself on the verge of tears and excused myself to the bathroom to hide it.

'Hey, I'll get a photo of you guys!' Melissa said as she lifted her iPhone. The last thing I wanted to do was sit next to him, let alone pretend to be cheerful for a photo.

'Are you okay, bub?' Mum asked. It must have been a mother's instinct because she could tell something was wrong.

'I'm fine,' I lied. 'I just have a headache.'

We left that evening in separate cars; I drove to our shoe box, and he drove to who-knows-where.

🏃 🏃 🏃

January 2013

'I want a divorce.'

It was New Year's Day, and his words came through my iPhone speaker devoid of emotion. And just like that, our marriage was over.

I didn't tell my parents until almost a week later. They were about to embark on their very first overseas holiday together, and the last thing I wanted to do was spoil their trip. But when I found out that he'd unfriended my entire family on Facebook, I knew it wouldn't be long before the truth came out. So I decided to tell Mum everything over cappuccinos at McDonald's.

'How could he do this to you?' she asked.

I wondered the same. Sure, our relationship was miles from perfect, but I loved him and believed he loved me in return.

I battled with the black dog following the separation, and it almost won. I remember sobbing as I ripped up photos of us from happier times. I blamed myself, convinced the fault was entirely mine. *If only I'd done x, y, and z, then he wouldn't have cheated on me*, I reasoned.

I'll forever feel blessed that I had my family to lean on during this time. Mum and Dad invited me to move back home with them until I could get back on my feet and afford a place of my own. I honestly don't know where I'd be without them. When I tell people I have the best parents in the world, I'm not just saying it — it's true!

My brother Daniel lived with my parents at the time. He always knew how to make me laugh, even when I was at my lowest. He may be seven years younger than me, but I've learned so much from him. He's such a mature, compassionate young man, and has a good head on his shoulders.

I only planned to stay there for six or so months. But it was impossible to leave a home full of so much love and support, and it took me two and a half years before I finally moved out!

I'm also incredibly grateful for the endless love and support from Melissa and Aurelle. They are without a doubt the best friends a girl could ever ask for. Barely a day goes by without us talking, usually via Facebook

Messenger because we're Millennials. When life threw this curveball, they were the first ones to offer listening ears.

February 2013

A couple of months after the separation, we met to discuss our impending divorce. I felt like I was sitting across from a stranger. He told me about his new girlfriend whom he'd met on New Year's Eve.

I'd already stalked her on Facebook, of course. She looked pretty in her photos, with deep brown eyes and a dazzling white smile. What did I hope to achieve by finding out everything I could about her? To feel better about myself? It only made me feel worse.

I wondered what it was about her that made him choose her over me. I knew I wouldn't be able to change his mind about the divorce; he didn't want to get back together with me. Did I even want him to? I wasn't sure if I'd ever be able to trust him again.

I'd lie in bed at night, re-reading the messages he'd written to the other women, trying to make sense of how our marriage had gone so wrong. Shadows danced across my bedroom walls, mirroring the storm raging inside me. The revelation of his betrayal pressed down on me like a heavy weight, and I didn't know how to lift it.

I closed my eyes and prayed, *Lord, I know I should forgive him, but I still feel so angry! Please help me.* With trembling hands, I opened my blush pink Bible, a beloved gift from my mentor and friend Lil when I first became a Christian. I read Ephesians 4:32: 'Be kind to one another, tenderhearted, forgiving one another, as God in Christ forgave you.' God showed me that I had the *choice* to forgive him, just as God Himself chose to forgive me.

My road to forgiving my ex-husband hasn't been a smooth one. The memories resurface at times, and I must confront and process the pain all over again. I've had to grapple with my own brokenness in being unwilling to extend the same grace that God has shown me. I sometimes take two steps forward, then one step back.

I've learned that the path to forgiveness, much like training for a marathon, requires perseverance. It's tempting to get caught up in chasing immediate results, but the endurance demanded by the distance is built graduallly over time. Being intentional and committing to each step of the process brings you closer to the finish line.

The important thing to remember is that progress is more important than perfection. I'm thankful that God continually gives me the strength I need to lift the burden of bitterness and resentment from my shoulders, replacing it with an indescribable sense of peace and freedom that can only come from Him.

CHAPTER 8

'Friendship is born at that moment when one person says to another, "What! You too? I thought I was the only one."'
—C.S. Lewis

19 September 2011 – 13 February 2013

The first time I met Geoff was awkward.

I'd landed my dream job as Writer — and later Child Sponsorship and Marketing Coordinator — for a small Christian non-profit organisation called WorldShare. I was thrilled to work for a charity that was passionate about transforming lives in the world's poorest regions through education, health, and sharing the good news of Jesus.

It's such a small world that the office was located in Five Dock in Sydney's inner west, just a few minutes' walk from my previous job as a medical receptionist. I lived in Holsworthy in Sydney's south-west at the time, and the last place in the world I wanted my new job to be was Five Dock because the travel time was almost two hours each way via public transport. But there was no way I could pass up this opportunity.

My heart fluttered with both nerves and excitement as I walked up the tiled white stairs to hand in my signed employment contract. I sensed tension in the air the instant I walked through the glass door.

'Hi, I'm Steph. I'm starting here next week. I'm just bringing in my contract.'

'I can take that,' said a dark-haired man in a salmon pink business shirt as he accepted the contract. He extended his other hand and introduced himself, 'I'm Geoff, the Finance Manager.'

Geoff's genuine smile and upright posture radiated confidence. I noted his soft hands, evidence of his status as a white-collar worker.

'And this is Judy.' Geoff gestured towards the lady who was sitting at the desk behind him. She ignored me completely, not looking up from her computer screen once. I later learned that she'd been made redundant from her role. And now here I was, the new girl on the block, taking over her position in a part-time capacity.

🏃 🏃 🏃

After I separated from my ex-husband in December 2012, Geoff and I spent more time together. We bonded over a mutual love of running, fluffy puppies, eighties music, vegetable juice, and, most importantly, our Christian faith. He was there for me through my darkest moments, and was always willing to offer advice or a shoulder to cry on. He had been through a divorce himself, so he understood from experience what I was going through.

Some of my 'friends' accused Geoff of taking advantage of me while I was 'vulnerable', but nothing could be further from the truth. Geoff is fifteen years older than me, so he'd call me his 'little sis'. I hated that! I wanted more; I wanted to be his girlfriend. But initially he didn't see me like that at all. I was the one who pursued a romantic relationship with *him*. In retrospect, I was nowhere near ready to jump into another relationship so soon after my first marriage ended, but I was in denial.

44

Growing up, I was often compared to my identical twin sister. People are naturally curious and fascinated by twins, particularly when it comes to the whole nature versus nurture debate. This led to me measuring myself against Melissa. Even though there was no one in the world more like me, I wanted to be more like her!

Melissa would usually get better results in her exams and assignments at school. She wouldn't beat me by much, but it was enough for me to be convinced that not only was she more intelligent than I was, but that I was 'stupid'.

I also remember a particular day when a family member told Melissa, 'You could be a model.' And from that day forward, I told myself that not only was she prettier than I was, but that I was 'ugly'.

Dumb, I know. I realise now how irrational my thinking was, but this constant comparison has had a significant impact on my self-esteem. Even to this day, I struggle to keep eye contact with others, even my closest friends and family. But with Geoff, it felt perfectly natural to gaze straight into his hazel eyes. I could be myself around him, without worrying what he thought of me.

And we had so much fun together! We'd muck around in the office, playing lightsaber wars by wielding giant rolls of fabric that were waiting to be shipped to WorldShare's ministry partner in the Democratic Republic of Congo. I found it amusing that not only do our names Geoff and Steph rhyme, but the names of our cars, Benny and Penny, did too. Surely it was meant to be!

It wasn't long before Geoff came up with a nickname for me — 'Cheekball.' He'd call me that when I said something cheeky. This eventually transformed into other nicknames, including CB, Ball of Cheek, BOC, Cheeseball, and Cheese. We use these nicknames for each other to this day.

When Geoff could see that my marriage was irreconcilable, he asked me to be his girlfriend. Our first official date was on the thirteenth of February

2013 at 360 Bar and Restaurant, a revolving restaurant atop Sydney Tower. We chose the day before Valentine's Day because we knew it wouldn't be as crowded. From eighty-eight stories above the ground, I savoured our fine dining experience with panoramic views of Sydney Harbour and the city.

Geoff and I would go for runs together around Five Dock, Canada Bay, and Cabarita during our lunch breaks. Our favourite spot was the popular 'Bay Run', a mostly flat seven-kilometre circuit around the picturesque Iron Cove Bay. We'd enjoy a post-run coffee and smoothie at Nield Park Pavilion — when we were lucky enough to get a table!

Geoff and I were the weird kind of couple who'd choose to go for a run over dinner and a movie for date night. Every weekend, we'd hop in Geoff's grey Nissan Micra and drive to the Blue Mountains to check out a new trail, or head to Palm Beach for a jog up the hill to Barrenjoey Lighthouse.

Geoff is much faster than I am, so he'd run ahead for a bit and then turn back to meet me again, or cut his own zig-zag path across the road ahead of me. I didn't mind too much because it gave me a chance to admire his tanned, chiselled calves, the result of his active northern beaches lifestyle.

When we weren't running ourselves, we'd park the Micra at Centennial Park in Sydney's eastern suburbs, losing track of time as we watched strangers navigate the 3.7-kilometre circuit. We'd recline our seats back and take turns analysing their form and technique, commenting on their stride length, arm swing, and posture. We'd guess what their pace was as they passed us, and eagerly await their return to see whose prediction was the closest.

23 July – 11 August 2013

As I stepped out of the hotel, I was hit by a stifling breeze that carried the scent of spices from the food vendors lining the sidewalks. Honking cars reluctantly slowed down to give way to a lone cow — considered a sacred animal in Indian religions such as Hinduism — that was meandering lazily through the dusty streets.

I was in Bengaluru (formally called 'Bangalore') in southern India for a work trip as part of my role at WorldShare. I'd registered for the upcoming City2Surf, so I needed to fit in as much last-minute training as possible.

I have never felt more unsafe during a run. In Australia, I've often been startled by the roar of an engine and indecipherable yells from hoons zipping by in their 'souped-up' cars. But this was something else. These are the thoughts that played over and over in my mind:

What am I doing out here? Is a personal best time worth putting my life in danger?

Why are all these people staring at me? Is it uncommon for people to run in India?

What if someone attacks me? I should have brought pepper spray…

Indian traffic is insane! I'm going to get hit by a car or a rickshaw or something.

Why didn't I ask one of my colleagues if they wanted to come for a run with me?

I didn't tell anyone I was going for a run. Who will know if something happens to me?

I should download one of those GPS tracking apps that tells my family where I am.

I should have taken a couple of self-defence classes.

I breathed a sigh of relief when I made it back to my hotel in one piece. My heart still racing from the adrenaline-fuelled run, I thanked God that he'd kept me safe. I decided that my next run should be on the hotel gym's treadmill — even if it meant death by boredom.

In the end, I wasn't even able to participate in the City2Surf because I came home sick with the dreaded Delhi belly!

During my time in India, I visited WorldShare's partner Bangalore City Mission, a ministry that shares Jesus' love with those living in the poorest areas of Bengaluru city. I had the opportunity to see the impact of child sponsorship firsthand. Now, when people ask why I'm so passionate about child sponsorship, I have a genuine answer — I've seen that it works!

I attended the morning assembly at Bangalore City Mission's Sinclairs School, where I was greeted by over six hundred smiling children in their red, yellow, purple, and green school uniforms. The girls in their double plaits were especially endearing. There was so much joy in the atmosphere as the children sang songs about Jesus and prayed together. I was so impressed with how well-behaved they were!

I had the privilege of meeting five-year-old Joshua, one of my own sponsored children. He was super shy at first — until I gave him an Aussie Rules football and did my best to teach him how to kick and pass it. The memory of Joshua laughing and jumping up and down as I blew bubbles will be something I'll always cherish.

I also visited the nearby Hosur Bande rock quarry. I saw people working in the scorching hot sun amid blasts from dynamite. Within ten minutes, my eyes were watering from the dust swirling in the air. *How do these poor people live like this?* I thought.

It was there I met a young boy I'll never forget. Sunil, no older than twelve years of age, had tousled black hair and downcast eyes. It broke my heart to hear his story. Sunil had watched his mother commit suicide by lighting herself on fire years earlier. Abandoned by his father, he was left to look after his younger brother on his own, and forced to do hard labour to meet their basic needs.

Things that children in Australia take for granted, like playing games and going to school, were nothing more than a dream for Sunil. And the only thing standing in the way of him having a bright future like little Joshua was someone's decision to sponsor him.

I returned home to Australia filled with a renewed sense of purpose, eager to share how child sponsorship can radically transform the lives of children in need.

CHAPTER 9

'[Ultramarathons are] eating and drinking contests,
with a little exercise and scenery thrown in.'
—Christopher McDougall

BIG RED RUN
DAY 2

3 July 2014

The Big Red Run begins and ends in Birdsville, an outback town sitting on the edge of the Simpson Desert where the borders of Queensland, South Australia, and the Northern Territory meet. At 1,590 kilometres west of Brisbane and 720 kilometres south of Mount Isa, Birdsville is, quite literally, in the middle of nowhere.

It had taken Dad and me two and a half days to travel here by car. I was thrilled when Dad first told me he was keen to come along as a volunteer. He might be a man of few words, but his actions speak volumes when it comes to going the extra mile to help his children — even if it means driving 1,912 kilometres to support one of us to run a crazy ultramarathon through the desert.

I loved every minute spent with Dad in his trusty Toyota Hilux, singing along to Kasey Chambers' album *Barricades and Brickwalls* and snacking on Allen's snake lollies. We cheered when we arrived in the little town of Nyngan on the first night of our road trip. With a population of 1,988, Nyngan is considered the 'gateway' to the outback in New South Wales. It was my first time visiting the vast, remote centre of Australia, and I was so excited about the adventure ahead of me.

I wake to the smell of fried eggs and toasted bread from the Birdsville Bakery. I struggle out of my sleeping bag, my legs stiff from running a full marathon yesterday. Dad is at the portable stove, boiling water to make me a much-needed mug of instant coffee.

I line up at the start line just before eight-thirty, wearing the same Big Red Run race shirt and pair of black adidas shorts I wore yesterday. The race organisers have provided one short-sleeved shirt and one long-sleeved shirt for each runner, and we're required to wear one of these at every stage of the race. I catch a whiff of stale body odour from the runners around me and become self-conscious about my own pungent smell.

The archway at the start line is emblazoned with the words, *Don't sweat the small stuff — do something big.* Red bunting flags line the exit from the camp. The deafening *bang* of the starter's gun sends us on our way. I have no idea what the day will bring, but I am ready to face whatever comes.

I've learned a valuable lesson after what happened yesterday. I need to test my blood glucose levels *before* each checkpoint. Then, if I'm having a hypo, I can quickly eat something before I arrive and have to wait for my levels to return to the target range. I stow my snacks and blood glucose meter in the pockets of the straps of my backpack so I have easy access to them.

I look down at my A4-sized course map. I see that the first checkpoint is nine kilometres in, so I check my blood glucose around the seven-kilometre mark. I'm feeling good, so I'm surprised to see the number *3.6* flash back at me on the screen.

I must be experiencing something called 'hypoglycaemic unawareness', which means I can't tell that my blood glucose is low. I don't have any of my usual warning signs of a hypo, like shaky hands or blurred vision. As unpleasant as hypo symptoms are, they are actually really useful! Without them, I'm oblivious to the need to take action to bring my blood glucose level back to a safe range.

I quickly devour an energy gel and slowly make my way to the first checkpoint. If I hadn't checked my blood glucose when I did, I might not have made it. Without realising I needed to eat something, I could have fainted. With no one nearby, I might have slipped into a coma without anyone noticing. It's a terrifying thought…

When I told friends I was planning to run a race in the Simpson Desert, many of them asked, 'Wow! How will you survive the heat?' Thankfully, it isn't the middle of January when temperatures soar into the forties and the desert is closed. The average maximum temperature in July is only twenty degrees Celsius, so the running conditions are surprisingly pleasant.

People also expect that the Simpson Desert is made up of nothing more than soft sand. But the terrain varies dramatically, with much of the Big Red Run course on firmer surfaces. I prepared for the race by spending most weekends with Geoff at his home in Collaroy on Sydney's northern beaches, over an hour each way from Wattle Grove. My training consisted of gruelling runs along the soft sand at Dee Why Beach and over the rocky trails of Manly Dam.

It's a challenge to navigate the gibber plains, a deep red layer of shiny stones of all shapes and sizes. Although the wind and rain — yes, it does rain in the desert! — have caused most of the pebbles to settle into a flat carpet, many still stand loose. Every step is precarious, and it's a miracle that I don't twist an ankle or dislocate my knee. I'm sure many of the runners would agree that the gibber plains are the most difficult terrain of the course.

There was little rainfall in the beginning half of this year, so the trees are grey and naked. Yet many plants are thriving in the harsh, dry conditions, covering the sand dunes, and binding them together with an extensive root system. Rugged cane grass is plentiful, as is the Big Red Runner's worst enemy, spinifex grass. These menacing, spiky shrubs scrape my bare legs and attach themselves to my socks. The lacerations sting as they meet my sweat and sunscreen.

Why am I doing this? At some point in every race I run, I question why I'm there. Sometimes it's right at the start when I'm feeling tired, having woken up at stupid o'clock after tossing and turning all night. Sometimes it's during those first few kilometres when my muscles haven't yet warmed up, and I wonder how I'll make it to the end.

But for every time I've asked myself whether running a race is worth the discomfort, the answer has always been 'Yes!' There's always going to be a certain degree of suffering in running; if there wasn't, then everyone would do it!

I remember to read Geoff's note for the second day at the fifteen-kilometre checkpoint:

> *During race day 2 — Never give up! Unless of course you're too tired or sore or hot or need a beer. That's totally understandable.*

I'm all those things, but I'm not ready to give up just yet. Despite the challenges, I run well, keeping a steady pace over the 21.1 kilometres. I cross the finish line in a time of 3:07:24, and place sixth out of nine Little Red Runners for the day.

Back at camp, I post a couple of sand dune selfies on my Facebook page, including one that perfectly captures a fly hovering above my head. I'm treated to a ride in the bright yellow event helicopter, included in the Big Red Run's early bird entry fee. Seeing the vastness of the outback from the air takes my breath away!

I have a bird's-eye view of the rich red gibber plains below me, neatly layered between rows of bright orange sand dunes. Trees and shrubs are sparsely scattered over the landscape, and a long dirt road stretches out as far as my eye can see. I'm disappointed that Dad can't join me on the helicopter. I'm convinced he's working harder than I am, and he deserves it way more than I do!

The temperature drops as the sun disappears. The runners, supporters, and volunteers huddle together around the campfire. Family and friends massage the runners, while race volunteers carry over hot drinks to save us from hobbling over to the urn. The heat of the flames warms our weary muscles as we share tales of the day.

The conversation turns to what led each of us to take part in the Big Red Run. Many are here because they've been personally affected by type 1 diabetes, whether because they have it themselves or they have a loved one who has it. Some are here because they're seasoned ultrarunners, wanting to add this to their already impressive list of races, while others want to see if they have what it takes to run or walk 150 or 250 kilometres across a desert.

One of the things I love about events like this is that they bring together people from all walks of life. You may have absolutely nothing in common — except your passion for running, that is — but you can learn so much from listening to the experiences of others. I believe ultrarunners share a mutual respect, based on the fact that they all have the courage to do something big.

CHAPTER 10

'marathon: (noun) A popular form of overpriced torture wherein participants wake up at ass-o-clock in the morning and stand in the freezing cold until it's time to run, at which point they miserably trot for an interval of time that could be better spent sleeping in and/or consuming large quantities of beer and cupcakes.'
—Matthew Inman

December 2012 – April 2013

I'd been progressively increasing my race distances. I could now comfortably run a half marathon of 21.1 kilometres — comfortably enough anyway — but I seriously doubted that I'd ever be able to run a full marathon of 42.195 kilometres. *Only super fit people run marathons and that will never be me,* I told myself.

But I thought about it a bit more. *What's stopping me from giving it a go?* When I realised I didn't have a good enough excuse, I knew it was time to tick 'run a marathon' off my bucket list.

I guess you could say marathon running is in my blood. Clinging to the promise of a better life, my Papou and Yiayia (or *grandfather* and *grandmother* in Greek) migrated to Australia from Greece in the early sixties. According to legend, in 490 BC, a young Greek soldier named Pheidippides ran twenty-five miles from the town of Marathon to Athens to share the good news that the Greek military had won the Battle of Marathon against the much larger Persian army. When he arrived, he shouted out 'Nike' which means *victory*, before dropping dead from exhaustion.

In 1896, at the first modern Olympic Games in Athens, a 'marathon' event was held to pay tribute to Pheidippides. Twenty-five runners conquered the 24.85-mile route that spanned from Marathon Bridge to the Olympic Stadium in Athens.

The marathon distance as we know it was established at the 1908 London Olympics. The British Royal family requested that the race begin at Windsor Castle and finish at the Olympic Stadium's royal box. The total distance was 26.2 miles, or 42.195 kilometres.

I decided that the mostly flat course at the Australian Running Festival in Australia's capital city, Canberra, would be perfect for my first marathon. Not having a clue what was involved in training for a marathon, I registered and carefully followed a sixteen-week program I found in *Runner's World* magazine.

I ran four or five times per week, making sure I didn't increase my distance by more than ten per cent per week to avoid injury. Most of these runs were at a relaxed pace so I still had enough breath to talk normally, while others were faster paced intervals and tempo sessions. My body adapted quite well to the training, and what once felt physically demanding became almost... easy.

In saying that, I didn't always jump out of bed in the morning and think, *Woohoo! I'm going for a run!* I found it challenging to be out on long, monotonous stretches of road for many hours without some kind of mental stimulation. So, during longer runs, I'd listen to either music or audiobooks, sometimes fiction and sometimes non-fiction, depending on my mood.

I'm often asked, 'What do you think about when you're running, Steph?' Simple answer: anything and everything! I think about what I'm going to order for brunch as a reward for completing a tough interval session. I plan out my strategy for the next event on my race calendar. I wonder how I'm going to find the time to meet the next work deadline.

I also pray when I run. Just like the 'Flying Scotsman' Eric Liddell, the Olympic sprinter whose life is chronicled in the 1981 film *Chariots of Fire*, 'When I run, I feel His pleasure.' For me, the time I spend running isn't simply 'me time' — it's an opportunity to experience a deeper intimacy with God.

As my feet rhythmically hit the pavement, I hear the Holy Spirit's gentle whispers to my heart: 'Be still, and know that I am God' (Psalm 46:10). I acknowledge that running is something God has designed me to do, and that it's a gift He has given me to enjoy.

11 April 2013

After work on Friday, Geoff and I drove the four and a half hours to Canberra in his mum Marcelle's white campervan. Our friends used to tell us we were 'living the dream' because we went on holidays so often. But the reason we could do that was because we were content to sleep in the back of a car for three weeks rather than spend three nights in a five-star hotel. We'd strive to save money wherever we could, even if it meant swapping a luxurious resort for a two-person tent.

Trying to save money almost backfired this time. Geoff wanted to find the cheapest fuel to fill up the campervan, and the price at the petrol station in Sutton was more than he was willing to pay.

'Cheekball, I don't think there are any petrol stations between here and Canberra, are there?' I asked.

'It's okay. We'll make it.'

But we didn't. Geoff kept driving and driving, our tank almost empty. We ended up having to turn around and drive back to Sutton.

We eventually made it to Canberra. We hadn't wasted a cent on booking a campsite of course, so we pulled up on a random street close to the start line of the race on King George Terrace.

Speaking of saving money, Geoff — being the creative accountant that he is — had figured out a way to score a free entry to the marathon for himself. He somehow convinced me to send an email to the race organisers telling them that I needed a 'support person' during the race because I have type 1 diabetes.

They kindly obliged. Geoff would wear a special supporter's race bib, but his time wouldn't be officially recorded. Although it was almost entirely untrue that I needed a support person, I was glad to have him there to carry my diabetes supplies and snacks. I admired his humble willingness to carry my bright pink backpack for me!

🏃 🏃 🏃

12 April 2013

On Saturday morning, the day before the marathon, Geoff raced in the ten-kilometre event. He wanted to qualify for the front start zone in that year's City2Surf, and did so with an impressive time of 47:34.

'I'm so proud of you!' I said as he completed his post-race stretches. I envy Geoff's dedication to stretching; I know it would make me a stronger runner, but I'd rather spend my time doing a million other things.

That night we pigged out on gigantic bowls of fettuccine carbonara at an Italian restaurant called Via Dolce. Looking around, I guessed that most of the dinners were carb loading for the marathon like us. Carb loading is a nutritional strategy that involves loading up on carbohydrates on the few days before a long endurance event. Carbs are stored as glycogen, a form of glucose, in the muscles. By maximising these stores, you can delay fatigue and improve performance.

I needed all the help I could get to finish this marathon, so I got on board the carb loading train. My blood glucose levels rode a wild rollercoaster as I injected a billion and one times the amount of insulin I normally would to cover the hundreds of extra grams of carbs I ate. I devoured so much food that a wafer-thin mint would have pushed me over the edge and made me explode.

CHAPTER 11

*'Each and every one of us can achieve anything that we set
our mind to, if we take it just one step at a time.'*
—Pat Farmer

13 April 2013

The morning of the marathon arrived. Geoff and I woke up at sunrise to
eat our brekkie of wraps with banana, peanut butter, and honey in the
back of the campervan. We hoped this would give us enough time for our
metabolism to work its magic so we wouldn't need to use the bathroom
during the race.

I was filled with pre-race jitters as I pulled on my black 2XU tights,
black adidas T-shirt, and fluoro pink ASICS shoes. *Am I ready for this? Have
I done enough to get to the finish line?* My longest run during my training was
thirty-six kilometres. That was a hard slog, and I wondered how I could run
an extra six kilometres on top of that.

Having no clue about optimum race nutrition, Geoff and I winged
it. We packed about half a dozen energy gels and a handful of jellybeans.
We'd also secretly stashed a big can of Monster energy drink beneath a park
bench at the thirty-kilometre mark the day before while we were scoping
out the course.

Looking back, I think Geoff probably ate a bit more fibre than his system could handle. Mere minutes before the race started, Geoff said, 'I'll meet you at the start line.'

'What?! What do you mean? Why can't you come with me now?'

I didn't have a chance to finish that question before Geoff was bolting down the street, calling out, 'Don't worry! I'll be there before the race starts.'

And then it dawned on me — Geoff needed to go to the toilet, and I don't mean a number one. As he darted around searching for a discreet place to relieve himself, his worst fears were realised. There were no bushes in sight, and his only option was to squat down next to a tree and do his business. There was nothing he could do to stop it; nature was calling.

Caught off guard by the sudden urgency, Geoff found himself without any toilet paper and resorted to a clump of grass. He sheepishly looked around as he pulled up his shorts and made his way over to me. Thankfully, there was no one around to witness any of it! Since that day, he has religiously carried his 'Bag of Hope' filled with toilet paper on every single run.

It wasn't the greatest start to our first ever marathon. We had just enough time to fit in our last-minute calf and quad stretches. The race commentator shouted over the loudspeaker, 'Put your hand up if this will be your first ever marathon.' We raised our arms and were pleased to see we weren't the only ones.

The anticipation in the atmosphere was palpable. All my training was behind me now. *Am I insane to think I can actually do this?* The gunfire sounded, and the usual snail pace walk to the timing mats commenced. This was it — the moment of truth. I was about to find out if I had what it takes to run 42.195 kilometres.

We began with a steady ascent up Capital Hill, looping around Parliament House with its iconic eighty-one-metre-high flag mast rising out of the landscape, before heading towards the glistening centrepiece of Canberra, the artificial Lake Burley Griffin.

There's no question that the toughest part of the course was the roughly five-kilometre out-and-back section along a desolate stretch of road that seemed to never end — and we had to run it twice!

The last person we expected to see running the race was Jesus. Okay, it wasn't *actually* Jesus. It was a random dude with a long brown wig, sporting nothing but a white loincloth and a crown of thorns. I was impressed that he ran the entire marathon barefoot!

That's one of the things I love most about running — you don't need much to get started. You don't need to buy special equipment like racquets, gloves, or helmets (unless you're particularly clumsy). You don't need to sign up for an expensive gym membership that you'll hardly use. You don't need perfect weather conditions because you can go out in the sun, wind or rain (hail might hurt though). Even shoes are unnecessary if you're part of the barefoot running community.

That said, there are additional items that can make running that little bit more comfortable, like waistbelts to hold your water, snacks, keys, and anything else you might need; ultralight, waterproof, wind-resistant jackets with advanced technology; bone conduction headphones that allow you to enjoy your favourite tunes while still being aware of your surroundings; and let's not forget GPS watches, which provide you with more workout stats than you'll know what to do with.

I had no inkling that my first marathon would become my first ultramarathon until I was running it.

The race announcer that morning had informed the runners that they could keep running once they finished the marathon, and go on to complete the ultramarathon if they wished to do so. An ultramarathon is any race longer than the traditional marathon length of 42.195 kilometres. This particular ultramarathon was fifty kilometres.

Throughout the race, Geoff and I joked about the idea of us doing it, without any real expectation that we could. 'We'll see how we go.' Well, I guess there's a reason Mum calls Geoff 'Forrest 1' and me 'Forrest 2'. That day, like Forrest Gump in the 1994 comedy film, we 'just felt like running.' We finished the marathon and kept going!

The last 7.8 kilometres felt like the slowest of my life. To put it in perspective, we finished the marathon in 4:40:06, averaging six minutes and thirty-eight seconds per kilometre — respectable enough for a first marathon. We completed the fifty kilometres in 5:50:00, averaging eight minutes and fifty-eight seconds per kilometre.

Because Geoff and I hadn't signed up for the ultramarathon in advance, we were wearing race bibs for the marathon. So, when we finally crossed the finish line, a crowd of volunteers had linked their fingers to form a tunnel *just for us*; they thought we were the last runners to finish the marathon!

But even intense embarrassment couldn't contain my smile as I 'sprinted' across the line, Geoff's hand in mine. I couldn't believe it; I'd run an ultramarathon! If someone had told me two years earlier, when I was struggling to run fifty metres at Moorebank hockey fields, that I'd one day be able to run fifty kilometres, I would have laughed and said, 'No way!'

Geoff shamelessly asked the event volunteers if we could have two race medals each — one for the marathon and one for the ultramarathon. He hadn't even paid for the race! But I have to say I'm glad he did because it was cool to get two medals. I certainly felt like I'd earned them.

I could barely walk for the next week. You would have laughed out loud if you'd seen me waddle downstairs like a penguin! But as Czech long-distance runner Emil Zátopek said at the end of one of his marathons, 'It was the most pleasant exhaustion I have ever known.' To describe crossing the finish line as 'awesome' would be an understatement.

Zátopek is best known for winning three gold medals at the 1952 Helsinki Olympics. After winning gold in the 5,000 and 10,000 metre races, he decided at the last minute to compete in the marathon. It was the first one he'd ever run, and he won!

Zátopek wasn't wrong when he said, 'If you want to run a mile, then run a mile. If you want to experience a different life, run a marathon.' There is no doubt about it — running a marathon had changed me. I finally realised that no matter how big my goals are, there's no reason I can't accomplish them. If I want to do something, all I need to do is set my mind to it and take one small step towards it at a time.

CHAPTER 12

'Trust in the LORD with all your heart, and do not lean
on your own understanding. In all your ways acknowledge
him, and he will make straight your paths.'
—Proverbs 3:5-6

11 February 2014

Shortly after my divorce had been finalised, I had a routine dental appointment. The lady behind the reception desk looked familiar. It took half a minute before it clicked — it was my ex-husband's new girlfriend!

Maybe I should have said something. But as anyone who knows me will tell you, I can be shy when I first meet someone. And what was I going to say? *Hey, I'm your boyfriend's ex-wife. Nice to finally meet you.*

I'm sure she knew who I was. I hadn't gotten around to changing my married name back to my maiden name yet. Surely that would have given it away, even if she hadn't seen a photo of me before. But if she did recognise me, she didn't say anything.

Most people hate going to the dentist, and for good reason. There's the rubbery smell of the latex gloves, the white napkin wrapped around your neck, the razor-sharp tools drilling into your gums, the interrogation about how often you floss, not to mention the exorbitant financial costs. Imagine adding to that having your ex-husband's new girlfriend's fingers in your mouth! It was the most uncomfortable experience of my life.

It's a shame, really; he was an excellent dentist.

14 – 25 March 2014

The evening began like any other. I arrived home from work at six, exhausted and ready to relax in front of the telly. But, as usual, my dogs Darcy and Chelsea were staring at me through the back door, waiting with wagging tails to go on a walk around the block. How could I say 'no' to them?

Like Chelsea, Darcy's exact breed remains a mystery. When I rescued him from an animal shelter in Wagga Wagga in 2008, a staff member said, 'This little guy was abandoned by his owner. We think he's a Chihuahua crossed with a Jack Russell, but we can't be one hundred per cent sure.'

Geoff and I were once stopped in the street by a dog breeder who excitedly told us that Darcy was 'definitely a Corgi.' I wasn't convinced. While he had the face and ears typical of a Corgi, his legs were taller.

About two kilometres into our usual four-kilometre loop around the streets of Wattle Grove, Darcy's leash slipped out of my hand. He bolted into the pitch black, and I lost sight of him. Okay, it wasn't *that* dark, but I have terrible night vision so it might as well have been. I strained my eyes to see what lay ahead of me. I wasn't sure which direction he'd gone, and I must have picked the wrong one because I couldn't track him down.

I searched and searched for close to an hour, calling out 'Darcy!' with no care for the families whose dinner time I might be disturbing. Hoping that Darcy would know how to make his own way back home, I completed the loop, with Chelsea still wagging her tail at a million miles an hour, oblivious to what had happened. I was distraught as I walked into the house. Dad did his best to reassure me as he drove me around the neighbourhood to look for Darcy.

My next step was to write a post on the local Facebook group for lost and found pets. The group's admin, Claire, was an experienced animal rescuer, and quickly offered to help me look for him the very next morning. I was overwhelmed by the kindness of countless people in the community who gave me advice, shared my Facebook post, scouted the streets, or dropped flyers in letterboxes. I was especially touched when my Uncle Jim offered a generous reward for Darcy's safe return.

I did absolutely everything I could think of to find Darcy. I annoyed the local council, vets, and animal shelters with phone calls every day. I printed off posters and flyers and distributed them throughout the neighbourhood. I walked for kilometres and kilometres each day, searching in shrubs, yelling out Darcy's name. I couldn't help but fear the worst. I kept picturing my little man lying helpless in a gutter somewhere. *Where could he possibly be?*

I thought back to when I first laid eyes on Darcy at the animal shelter. He was in a room of his own because he was less than three months old and hadn't been vaccinated yet. He was a bundle of energy, with big eyes and pointy ears that were disproportionately larger than the rest of his tiny face. I fell in love with him instantly, and knew there was no way I could go home without adopting him.

26 March 2014

Twelve agonising days after Darcy went missing, I had a revelation that became one of the most profound lessons of my life. I was convicted that I hadn't been trusting God and His will for me and Darcy. Instead of asking Him to help me find Darcy, I'd been trying to do everything in my own strength.

I decided to quit running around like a headless chicken, and went running back to God. I remembered His promise in Philippians 4:6-7: 'Do not be anxious about anything, but in everything by prayer and supplication with thanksgiving let your requests be made known to God. And the peace of God, which surpasses all understanding, will guard your hearts and your minds in Christ Jesus.' As I prayed, a profound sense of peace washed over me as I put Darcy in God's hands.

The sun had already set when I arrived home from work later than normal that night. I watched Chelsea through the kitchen window. She was laying on the table in the backyard, not her usual excitable self. I've never met a dog more enthusiastic about going for walks than Chelsea is. I call her the 'Forrest Gump of dogs' because if I were to let her run for as long as she pleased, I don't think she'd ever stop! You'd never know from looking at her that she had major surgery on her back knees when she was a puppy. The vet must have replaced them with bionic bones. It was heartbreaking to see her look so lost without her bestie.

It was raining cats and dogs, and the last thing I wanted to do was go for a run. Mum almost talked me out of it too. 'You can't go running now! It's so late!' But the Big Red Run was only fourteen weeks away, and I couldn't afford to make excuses this late in the game. So I laced up my running shoes and set off into the night.

About half a kilometre from my house, I ran past a side street on my left just as a lady emerged from it with a dog on a leash. I ran a metre or so past them when it occurred to me that it wasn't just any dog — it was *my* dog! I stopped dead in my tracks, hardly able to believe my eyes.

'Did you find that dog?!' I exclaimed, more a statement than a question.

'Um, yes, I did. Is he yours?'

'Yes!'

Darcy wagged his tail wildly as I bent down to pat him. When he jumped all over me and gave me enthusiastic doggy kisses, there was no way the lady could deny he was mine.

'I was minding him. I was planning to take him to the vet tomorrow,' she said.

I was sure she must be lying. My guess is that Darcy was heading home the night he went missing, only to be intercepted along the way. I'd put up posters in that very street, and the lady would have to have been blind not to notice them. She mustn't have wanted to be seen with the easily recognisable Darcy, which explains why she was walking him in the cover of darkness. I also noticed that Darcy was sporting a brand-new, shiny red collar instead of the ragged blue collar he had on in the photo on the posters.

Needless to say, I didn't give the lady Uncle Jim's reward money! I raced straight home with the biggest grin on my face and tears streaming down my flushed red cheeks. Darcy and I were finally reunited, and I couldn't have been happier. After twelve days away, my baby boy was home.

$$\text{🏃 🏃 🏃}$$

7 April 2014

To celebrate Darcy's safe return and to thank everyone who had helped look for him, I organised a welcome home party at Wattle Grove Lake. Everyone, including the dogs, wore party hats. Together we drank champagne and enjoyed my new friend and fellow dog lover Peta's delicious chocolate cupcakes, with icing carefully crafted into the shape of Darcy's face.

The local newspaper, *Liverpool Leader*, was there to cover the story of how the community had come together to look for Darcy. He didn't know it, but he'd become the most famous dog in the neighbourhood.

Finding Darcy wasn't a coincidence; it was a miracle! Nothing else could explain the fact that *I* was the one who found him in such an unlikely way, when so many others had also been looking for him. On the very day I learned the important lesson to trust God in the situation, *Bam!* Darcy turned up. God had put me in just the right place at just the right time.

CHAPTER 13

*'God cannot give us happiness and peace apart from Himself,
because it is not there. There is no such thing.'*
—C.S. Lewis

August 2014

Geoff broke up with me a month after the Big Red Run. We'd been together for eighteen months and I thought it was the natural next step that we get married. The problem was I simply didn't know how to let go of *needing* him to propose. All I was doing was putting pressure on him, which only led to me pushing him further and further away.

To say I was upset about the breakup would be the understatement of the century. The world around me faded into a haze as waves of despair crashed over me. It felt like the earth had been ripped from beneath my feet. I was so confused because I was *convinced* that God's plan was that Geoff and I would get married. *How can Geoff not see that?*

I was driving home from work one evening when Whitney Houston's song 'All At Once' streamed through the radio. The lyrics spoke about the sudden realisation of a relationship breakdown and the finality of it all.

And that's when it hit me — it was over. I had to pull over because tears blurred my vision. Geoff is a diehard Whitney fan (sorry for sharing your secret, Cheekball!), and I held onto memories of singing her songs with him at the top of our lungs.

We were still working together at WorldShare at the time, our desks only a metre apart. To avoid any awkwardness, we had to plan the days we worked from home so that we saw as little of each other as possible.

The downsides of an office romance, right? It's great when everything's smooth sailing; but if you hit an iceberg, it's probably a wise idea to jump ship.

11 – 15 November 2014

Shortly before the breakup, Geoff and I had booked flights to New Zealand for a ten-day holiday. The main reason for the trip was that Geoff was going to be a groomsman at a friend's wedding. I thought I would be a bit out of place there, so I made the tough decision to stay in Australia.

I already had annual leave approved, so I figured I might as well escape the hustle and bustle of Sydney. I was tossing up between driving up or down Australia's east coast. I finally settled on spending five days at Thredbo in the heart of Kosciuszko National Park, near the border between New South Wales and Victoria.

I'd never seen snow in Australia before. Although it was the end of Spring, I took the chance that there might still be snow there when I arrived. As the wheels of my bright pink-purple Mitsubishi Mirage rolled down the highway, I enjoyed belting out my favourite tunes without fear of judgement.

I didn't have any upcoming races planned, but I wanted to maintain my fitness while I was away. I had not one, but *two* near-death experiences on my first run. I pulled over at Lake Crackenback on the way to Thredbo to make the most of the day's little remaining sunlight. I was ten kilometres into the run when I took a wrong turn. Daylight was fading, and my iPhone battery was almost dead.

I sat down on a rock to assess the situation. There wasn't much point in taking out my compass because, to be perfectly honest, I didn't have any idea how to use it. I heard a loud rustling behind me, and jumped up in time to spot a two-metre-tall Eastern Grey Kangaroo bounding towards me.

If I'd stood up even a second later, the kangaroo wouldn't have seen me in time to stop. It would have toppled over me, crushing me under its giant paws, and I would have been seriously injured. I think it was as frightened as I was when it spotted me!

I had my second near-death experience minutes later. I'd worked out roughly which direction I should be heading, and was running again. I couldn't see far ahead of me because it was getting dark. I ended up just a couple of feet away from an Eastern Brown Snake! I let out a gasp as I narrowly missed stepping on the second most venomous snake in the world.

I was relieved when I made it back to my car. I drove twenty minutes to my accommodation in Thredbo, the cheapest hostel I could find because I was broke after spending all my savings on the New Zealand trip. I was worried I'd have to share my room with others when I walked in and saw bunk beds, but thankfully it was low season so I had the entire room to myself.

The next morning, I took an express chairlift to the start of the track leading to the top of Mount Kosciuszko, Australia's tallest mountain at 2,228 metres. The thirteen-kilometre return walk was much easier than I'd anticipated, taking less than three hours to complete.

Slippery cold sludge covered sections of the track, so my dream of seeing snow in Australia finally became a reality — though trudging through it wasn't quite the magical experience I'd imagined.

The Black Screen of Death appeared on my iPhone one hundred metres from the summit. *Oh man, I won't have photos to prove I've been to the top!* I thought. *Oh wait, it'll be on Strava.* It was an awesome feeling knowing I was higher than any other person on the continent of Australia at that moment.

🏃 🏃 🏃

November 2014 – March 2015

During my time in Thredbo, I delved into the classic novel, *Robinson Crusoe* by Daniel Defoe. The following passage challenged me: 'Those people cannot enjoy comfortably what God has given them because they see and covet what He has not given them. All of our discontents for what we want appear to me to spring from want of thankfulness for what we have.'

I had the revelation that although my relationship with Geoff hadn't worked out the way I'd hoped, I still had so much to thank God for! Seeking a fresh start, I got stuck into reading God's Word, and asked Him to give me wisdom for the next chapter of my life.

Even still, I was living in the shadow lands. I pursued relationships with other men after Geoff broke up with me. How many? Well, let's just say I need at least one hand to count. These men would profess their love for me, and I would echo it, but only because I didn't want to hurt them if I didn't reciprocate.

I was running away from God, chasing a happiness hinged on the success of my love life, ignoring the fact that such a happiness doesn't exist! I feared being alone, forgetting that God had already promised He would never leave me nor forsake me (Deuteronomy 31:8). I regret breaking hearts in the process.

As I prayed, the Holy Spirit showed me that it was futile to seek fulfilment in worldly pleasures rather than in His perfect, unconditional love. And just like the prodigal son in Luke 15:11-32, who returned home in search of forgiveness, I turned back to God. Just like the father who ran to embrace his wayward son, my heavenly Father welcomed me with arms wide open, ready to forgive me and restore our broken relationship.

CHAPTER 14

*'In running, it doesn't matter whether you come in first,
in the middle of the pack, or last. You can say, 'I have
finished.' There is a lot of satisfaction in that.'*
—Fred Lebow

22 March 2015

The worst race performance of my adult life unfolded at the 2015 Sydney Trail Series. The race was set in Manly Dam, an extensive, tranquil bushland valley containing Sydney's largest freshwater lake.

I had a choice between the ten, twenty-one, and thirty-kilometre courses. Of course I chose the longest distance. I was looking forward to a mix of technical single tracks, wide fire trails, lakeside boardwalks, waterfalls, and native flora and fauna.

I'd been running four or five times per week, and my training was paying off. I was seeing improvements in my times, so I felt confident on race morning. Even though I wasn't with Geoff anymore, I did many of my long runs on the trails of the northern beaches. I also ran during my lunch breaks around Five Dock, or in the evenings after a long day at work around Wattle Grove.

The race started well, and I was optimistic that I'd get a result I was happy with. I was only four kilometres into the race when my blood glucose levels plummeted. I'd eat a snack to bring them up again, but it wouldn't be enough to prevent the next hypo.

I can't remember much of the race because having a severe hypo can be kind of like getting drunk, where you struggle to remember details of events. Back in high school, I apparently told a boy I had a crush on him while I was having a hypo. I don't think I even liked him at all, but he ended up asking me out and became my first boyfriend!

I was faint and dizzy from about nine kilometres into the race. I lost my balance so many times, tripping over twice — first on a tree branch, and then on jagged rocks leading down to the water's edge. I felt disillusioned when I reached each checkpoint, knowing I was coming dead last and that the race volunteers pitied me.

I dreaded seeing the letters *DNF* alongside my name on the official race results, so I kept going. And you know what? I learned one of the most important lessons that running has ever taught me: Humility.

When you become a runner, there will be days when nothing goes right. You'll be forced to pull out of a race due to injury. You'll trip over the timing mats and stack it at a finish line (something I did at another thirty-kilometre trail race on the Gold Coast!). You'll finish a race in last place, or much further down the ladder than you expected.

But I truly believe that humility is a good thing! It helps us recognise our own weaknesses and limitations, presenting us with the opportunity to cultivate resilience. In life, obstacles are inevitable; but when you stumble, you must choose to get back up and keep running the race.

I ran across the thirty-five-metre-high concrete dam wall and crossed the finish line. I could have given up *so* many times during the race, but I didn't. I never want to use my type 1 diabetes as an excuse. It makes every race that much more of an accomplishment, especially the ones that don't quite go to plan.

Do I think I'd be a faster runner if I didn't have type 1 diabetes? I don't know. And maybe I never will. When I was first diagnosed, Dad told me there would be a cure for type 1 diabetes by the time I was eighteen; this is what the media and my doctors told him. But, thirty-one years on, there is still no cure. Nevertheless, as I watch each breaking news story about a promising new trial on the five o'clock news, I hold out hope that one day there will be.

I've asked God countless times to take away my type 1 diabetes. I do believe that God heals people; however, I also believe that we must never presume that He *must* do so. Sometimes He allows us to experience suffering in order to teach us lessons we wouldn't be able to learn in any other way.

In 2 Corinthians 12:7-9, Paul pleaded with God to remove his 'thorn' on three occasions. God replied, 'My grace is sufficient for you, for my power is made perfect in weakness.'

In the same way, God hasn't fixed my pancreas (yet!), but His grace is more than enough to sustain me through any hardship I face. I'm confident that God is working through my type 1 diabetes for His ultimate glory.

27 March – 11 April 2015

In March 2015, I participated in a three-day, intensive personal development program. Geoff had been encouraging me to enrol in it for years, but I'd never felt ready. I'm so grateful that I finally made the commitment because it completely transformed my life.

The program encourages participants to identify and confront their fears, limiting beliefs, and patterns that are holding them back. The biggest breakthrough I had there was learning to let go of *needing* a relationship with Geoff. I realised that if I genuinely loved Geoff, I had to let him go.

After our breakup, I played Switchfoot's song 'Enough to Let Me Go' on repeat. The chorus poses the question, *Do you love me enough to let me go?* It wasn't until I did the program that the meaning of the lyrics dawned on me. True love doesn't mean *taking* from the other person, but rather *giving* to them. And sometimes what you need to give them is space, even when it's painful for you.

Geoff gave me a lift home after the final evening of the program, and I eagerly shared everything I'd learned.

'Cheekball, I love you so much, and I'm so sorry for putting so much pressure on you to propose. I'm still sad that we're not together, but I'm finally ready to let you go.'

And I was. I didn't have any expectation that we'd get back together. But this was all Geoff needed to hear to know that he wanted me to be his girlfriend again.

On the eleventh of April, Geoff and I had our second first date at The Little Snail, a super fancy French restaurant in Pyrmont. I dressed up in a blue and white floral mini dress, and even had my hair styled with waves by a hairdresser, something I only ever do for special occasions. (Let's face it — Geoff probably didn't even notice my effort!)

Over an entrée of escargot, we started planning our wedding. We both knew that if we ever got back together that we'd be getting married, so why put it off any longer?

CHAPTER 15

'Run when you can, walk if you have to, crawl
if you must; just never give up.'
—Dean Karnazes

25 April 2015

My first one hundred-kilometre ultramarathon was the Anzac Day Challenge. I couldn't think of a more significant way to mark one hundred years since Australian and New Zealand troops had landed in Gallipoli during the First World War than by running one hundred kilometres through Sydney's spectacular Ku-ring-gai Chase and Garigal National Parks.

I had just over three months to prepare. Living in Wattle Grove made it tricky to train for what was supposed to be a course with plenty of elevation. The paved paths of the south-west Sydney suburb are as flat as a pancake, so I ran many of my long runs at Manly Dam. I loved the trails there because they're brutal yet beautiful, and their solitude helped me leave behind Sydney's rat race.

A week before the Anzac Day Challenge, severe storms caused damage to large sections of the course. I was disappointed when I read an email from the organisers stating that they'd been forced to move the event to St

Ives Showground. Rather than running through picturesque scenery, we'd now have to run 155 laps around an oval!

The new format would undoubtedly be physically easier than one hundred kilometres on the trails, but there was no question that it would come with its own set of challenges. I never would have willingly signed up for a race like that; I couldn't think of anything more boring than running around and around the same track all day!

But I was committed. The Anzac soldiers who went to battle to serve their country didn't have a choice — they simply went. I knew I had it so easy in comparison to what they'd gone through, and I was prepared to face this monumental physical and mental challenge in their honour.

The insistent pings of my iPhone alarm startled me awake at four o'clock on race morning. Mum and I arrived at St Ives Showground just in time for the Anzac Day dawn service. Mum had come along to support me and the other participants as a race volunteer, just as Dad had done at the Big Red Run. She helped by cutting up watermelon and filling paper cups with water and electrolytes.

As the crowds gathered, I noticed many of the friends I'd made during the Big Red Run. There were ten of us altogether, and I was thrilled for another chance to experience the camaraderie we'd shared during our week in the Simpson Desert the previous year.

Mum was ecstatic when event ambassador 'Commando Steve' Willis, one of Australia's most recognised and respected (not to mention good-looking) health and fitness experts, arrived with his then-girlfriend, fellow personal trainer Michelle Bridges.

Never one to contain her excitement, Mum yelled out, 'We love you, Steve!' I don't know if I've ever seen a bigger smile on Mum's face than when I took a photo of them together.

Just before seven, 242 people huddled at the start line, 175 of whom would be tackling the one hundred kilometres solo, while the others would run as part of a two or three-person relay team. Many of the participants had personally been affected by war, whether they were soldiers themselves, had loved ones currently fighting overseas, or had retired from the armed forces due to physical or mental trauma. The event raised nearly $130,000 for Soldier On and Mates4Mates, two not-for-profit organisations that were supporting people like them.

We began with renditions of the Australian and New Zealand national anthems, followed by the Ode of Remembrance and a one-minute silence to honour the Anzacs. Commando Steve delivered a motivational speech to spur us on before firing the gun.

The mental toughness of the Anzac Day Challenge was far greater than what I'd anticipated coming into the race. Unlike the Big Red Run where the landscape changed endlessly, the flat, dirt track of St Ives Showground was monotonous. When Geoff arrived mid-morning, I was relieved to finally have pleasant scenery to enjoy.

I had no idea where everyone else was placed; the faster runners lapped me, while I overtook the slower runners and walkers. I was truly running my own race. Strangely, I've never felt more alone than I did on that run. Although there were hundreds of people around me, I was so in my own head and wrestled with self-doubt. *Can I finish before the twenty-four-hour cut-off time?*

An advantage of the course change was that the Big Red Runners had a designated gazebo where we could leave our food and other gear. I didn't have to carry anything, and I could stop whenever I needed to take a break.

One of the only respites from the tediousness of running 155 laps around an oval was the occasional change in direction from clockwise to anticlockwise (and vice versa) every few hours. Commando Steve's warm smile at the end of each lap also lifted my spirits, reminding me that the reason I was there was for Australians like him who have sacrificed so much for our country.

I listened to music to keep myself entertained. Mötley Crüe's 'Kickstart My Heart' took my mind off the dullness of my surroundings. Survivor's 'Eye of the Tiger' helped me to stay strong and not give up. TobyMac's 'Eye On It' encouraged me to press on with my eye on the prize.

My muscles screamed as each lap merged into the next. I went from a six-minute per kilometre running pace to a thirteen-minute per kilometre walking pace. Geoff and Mum had their own tag team and took turns doing laps with me. Geoff did at least fifty laps, and I'm sure Mum must have done at least twenty.

Mum epitomises the typical soccer mum, always present on the sidelines to support her three children. She's so proud of us and makes sure that everyone she meets knows it. Having her there to cheer me on after every lap meant so much to me, especially in the tough moments when I insisted, 'I can't do it, Mum!' She was with me every step of the way, reminding me that I could.

I was too nauseous to eat anything most of the day. I fought to keep food down, and only ate because I *had* to rather than because I *wanted* to. My blood glucose levels were high every time I checked them. I knew I needed to eat something to give me the fuel I needed to run, but the thought of it made me want to throw up.

About seventy kilometres in, my stomach felt settled enough to tolerate food again. I collapsed into a fold-out camping chair and gulped down two cups of steaming chicken and noodle soup.

Grey clouds rolled in by late afternoon, greeting us with torrential rain that hit us like ice. Each lap became excruciatingly more difficult. The temperature had plunged, and it wasn't long before I was shivering from head to toe.

I was suffering from hypothermia; my body was doing its best to protect itself from the cold, but I was losing heat faster than I was producing it. I wore my black gloves, my arctic blue rain jacket, and Geoff's black beanie. My friend Izzi, who'd already finished the race, kindly lent me a thermal shirt to wear. But no matter how many layers of clothing I put on, I couldn't get warm.

Lightning exploded in the sky above as rain continued to pelt down. *Maybe I can swim the last forty laps*, I thought. I was emotional from lack of sleep, wanting nothing more than to curl up like a burrito right there on the track and sleep through to the next morning.

'Go Cheekball! You can do it!'

Geoff's voice brought me back to reality. I'd covered seventy-five kilometres, so there was only one-quarter to go. *Yes, I can do it!* I thought. My quads throbbed, and a sharp pain coursed through my right knee. It took every bit of my willpower to push on.

As the night wore on, I felt more and more guilty that my support crew, particularly Mum and Geoff, were waiting in the rain and cold for me to finish. When the other Big Red Runners had completed the race, they could have easily gone straight home to shower and sleep. But many of them stuck around to make sure I finished my race too, reflecting the remarkable Anzac spirit of mateship and never leaving anyone behind.

At 1:07 am, just over eighteen hours since Commando Steve had fired the starting gun, I crossed the finish line — the same line I'd crossed 155 times that day. I was drenched and shaking like a leaf, but nothing could wipe the smile off my face. Mum was jumping up and down, her elated cheers echoing through the crisp air. The rain had transformed her once voluminous wavy brown hair into a cascade of damp strands.

The event organisers handed each of the finishers a Flanders poppy to place into a makeshift wall of remembrance. These striking scarlet flowers were among the first plants to bloom in the devastated battlefields of France and Belgium, and have become a powerful symbol of the sacrifice of the Anzac soldiers whose blood was spilled during the First World War.

You might be wondering what it takes to run one hundred kilometres in a day. Is there a secret? Not really. It's obvious that you can't expect to run that far without putting in the time and effort to physically prepare yourself for it. You need to commit to running crazy long distances, steadily increasing up to ten hours per week; it's basically a part-time job! You need to practise with the nutrition and the gear you plan to use on race day, and you need to train on a similar terrain to what you'll face during the event.

Someone who knows a lot about running one hundred-kilometre ultramarathons is American runner Jim Walmsley. In January 2021, Jim came agonisingly close to setting the world record in Arizona, covering the distance in 6:09:26 — just twelve seconds shy of the record set by Japanese runner Nao Kazami in 2018. That's *twelve hours* faster than my time at the Anzac Day Challenge!

Jim says, 'Ultrarunning doesn't take special talent. It takes motivation and the will to achieve something extraordinary.' You don't have to be a superhero to run an ultramarathon; they're run by ordinary people like me who have discovered the pure joy that comes with seeing how far we can go.

Remember the children's fable about the tortoise and the hare? The hare boasts about how fast he can run, mocking the tortoise for being so slow. Tired of hearing him brag, the tortoise challenges the hare to a race. The hare quickly leaves the tortoise in his tracks.

Confident that he'd win, the hare takes a nap under a tree midway through the race. But when the hare wakes up and reaches the finish line, he discovers that the tortoise is already there!

This mirrors the true story of Cliff 'Cliffy' Young, who is best known for his unexpected win in the inaugural Sydney to Melbourne Ultramarathon in 1983. At sixty-one years of age, the Aussie potato farmer showed up at the start line in a pair of overalls and rubber gumboots.

Cliffy ran 875 kilometres at a tortoise-like pace, and was well and truly in last place at the end of the first day. But while the other competitors stopped for six hours to sleep, Cliffy kept going. He shuffled along for five days straight, taking the lead during the first night and ultimately winning by a margin of ten hours!

The key to running one hundred kilometres is to pace yourself. It's perfectly acceptable to take walking breaks during an endurance event. Some might see it as a failure — that it means you're not a 'real' runner — but even elite runners know it's a wise strategy. A 2014 study in the *Journal of Science and Medicine in Sport* found that incorporating regular walking breaks can get you across the finish line at a similar time as those who run the entire way, while doing less damage to your body.

A one hundred-kilometre ultramarathon is not a hundred-metre sprint. Slow and steady wins the race — or at least gets you to the finish line if you're an average runner like me.

CHAPTER 16

'We'll always be together; Together in electric dreams.'
—Philip Oakey and Giorgio Moroder

13 May 2015

One month after we got back together and began planning our wedding, Geoff and I were on our favourite local running route. Starting at his home in Collaroy Plateau, it heads down the hill to busy Pittwater Road, around the beautiful, ocean-hugging Long Reef headland, and back home up the hill. Although it's only six kilometres, the up-and-down course is challenging.

We set out like any other evening, chatting about our day at work. Three kilometres in, we reached the top of the sandstone cliff facing the Pacific Ocean. We stopped to catch our breath and take a quick drink from the bubbler, soaking up the familiar sight of the waves crashing against the rocky shore below.

'It's a nice night. Why don't we get a photo?' Geoff asked.

I knew immediately that something was up because Geoff isn't usually keen to have his photo taken. He walked over to a middle-aged couple who stood arm-in-arm enjoying the uninterrupted ocean views. I couldn't hear what Geoff was saying as he handed them his phone, but I assumed he was asking them to take a photo of us (I found out later that he'd asked them to take a video).

As the sun set over the coastline, Geoff dropped to one knee and asked, 'Are you sure you want to marry me?'

He reached into his hideous neon yellow, bright pink, aqua blue, and black striped board shorts — which I've since thrown in the bin, certain even the Salvos wouldn't accept them — and pulled out the most stunning engagement ring with two Celtic love knots on either side of a flawless round diamond.

Of course I said, 'Yes!'

Well, to be honest, it's a bit of a blur so maybe I didn't, but he took my reaction as a 'Yes.' We were officially engaged. I had to wait a little while for it to happen, but I think the proverb, 'Good things come to those who wait,' is true because I'd never been happier than I was at that moment. Geoff couldn't have proposed in a more perfect way.

As we ran back up the hill, I kept my eyes fixed on my ring which sparkled in the last light of the day.

13 June 2015

Our wedding date was exactly one month after Geoff's proposal. This didn't exactly leave me much time to buy a wedding dress! But with Melissa's help, we managed to find my dream dress at the first store we visited. It was a magnificent white ballgown with a lace bodice and tulle skirt. We both knew as soon as I tried it on that it was the one, and I said 'yes' to the dress.

Geoff and I seriously considered getting eloped overseas. During our time working at WorldShare, we'd formed a friendship with Pastor John

Wandera, who runs a charity in Uganda called Christian Fellowship Ministries. It wouldn't have been nearly as stressful for us to get married there, but I'm so glad we changed our minds. It meant so much to be able to share our special day with twenty-four of our family members and friends.

The last thing I did before heading out the door for the wedding ceremony was to put on my shoes. I recall Mum's look of sheer horror when I pulled out a pair of pink and blue Skechers running shoes from the wardrobe.

'Oh, are you going to put your good shoes on when you're in the car?'

'Um, no Mum.'

'What do you mean?'

'I mean these are the shoes I'm wearing today.'

'You're not serious, are you?'

'Yes, I'm very serious,' I laughed.

Mum's mouth dropped open, reminding me why I didn't tell her beforehand. Geoff and I had decided to wear running shoes on our wedding day — a nod to our mutual love of running and the fact that our friendship had initially developed through the sport.

Besides, who wants to struggle to walk, let alone dance, in heels on what is supposed to be the best day of their life? Not me! Mum has since told me that it makes sense to her now.

Despite light rainfall the previous day, we had perfect weather on our wedding day. We had a beautiful outdoor ceremony at Long Reef Golf Club, overlooking Fishermans Beach at Collaroy, about one kilometre from the spot Geoff had proposed to me. I was so carefree as Dad walked me down the aisle towards my best friend — comfortably, thanks to my choice of shoes!

When Geoff and I said our wedding vows that day, we committed to a lifetime of running the race together, enjoying the adventure en route to Heaven.

In the world of running, there are three letters that you don't want to see next to your name on a list of race results: *DNF*, which stands for 'Did Not Finish'. My first marriage was a DNF. I think I'd entered it with a pie-in-the-sky vision of what it would be like. I pictured a fairytale happily ever after with my prince charming.

But the reality is that a successful marriage is a marathon, not a sprint. It requires a solid commitment and a heck of a lot of hard work. It's a journey that goes the distance, 'until death do us part'. While it can feel long, hilly, bumpy, scary, and exhausting, the sacrifices you make will be worth it!

When a runner signs up for a marathon, it's crucial that they train for the race. Running 42.195 kilometres is no walk in the park; you can't expect to get to the finish line if you don't put in the time and effort.

In the same way, we cannot become complacent in a marriage. We must stay consistent, never making excuses like, 'It's all too hard!' As 1 Corinthians 13:7 says, 'Love bears all things, believes all things, hopes all things, *endures* all things' (emphasis added).

18 – 30 June 2015

Geoff and I booked our honeymoon before we arranged anything else for our wedding, even the reception venue. We stumbled upon an unbelievably cheap last-minute cruise deal that we couldn't ignore. Five days after the wedding, we set sail on a thirteen-night Carnival cruise to the idyllic South

Pacific islands of Fiji, New Caledonia, and Vanuatu. It worked out costing less than fifty dollars each per night, including all the food we could eat!

A highlight of our honeymoon was our day on the Isle of Pines, an island paradise described as the 'Jewel of the Pacific'. We hired a couple of rusty ancient bikes from a tourist resort, and cycled twenty-two kilometres from one side of the island to the other. We could have paid to take a bus; however, having recently resigned from our jobs, we were both unemployed, and determined to stay that way for as long as possible.

We rode to a natural aquarium where we snorkelled among a vibrant kaleidoscope of fish in calm, crystal clear waters. A bright orange and white clownfish I named 'Nemo' bit me, but that was my own fault because I tried to touch him. This little expedition ended abruptly when Geoff pointed out a couple of bluebottles a metre from where we were swimming.

We were never bored on the cruise ship itself. We enjoyed live shows, played mini golf, tackled Sudoku puzzles, battled it out in trivia competitions, pushed around giant chess pieces, and swam laps in one of the pools.

We went for several runs, sometimes in the gym looking out across the wide blue ocean, and other times outdoors on the top deck of the ship. The rocky seas made it impossible for us to stand upright on the treadmills, and we didn't know how far our outdoor runs were because the moving ship rendered our GPS watches useless.

The wait staff entertained us in the dining hall every night. They'd get us up to dance to 'Nutbush City Limits', 'YMCA', or 'Macarena'. A lanky magician in a suit wandered around the ship doing magic tricks. One night he joined our dining table and performed some mind-blowing illusions. He placed a deck of cards in Geoff's palm, directing him to cover them with his other hand.

The magician moved a few feet away to perform a different trick for another couple. When he returned, he said, 'Lift your hand.' Geoff did so, revealing not a deck of cards, but a clear rectangular prism! How he managed to pull it off baffles us to this day.

Midway through the cruise, we went to the main auditorium to watch a live game show called 'The Love Boat' or something lame like that. The host of the show picked three couples from the audience to take part in the show. The first was an adorable elderly couple who'd been married for over half a century. The second was a young couple with two children.

The host announced, 'Next I want to bring up the newest newlyweds!'

Geoff and I looked at each other, thinking that it could well be us. We reluctantly raised our hands at the same time as another couple did. I'd lost track of days since being on the cruise, but before long the matter was settled — our wedding was the most recent. Hundreds of our fellow passengers cheered us on as we approached the stage.

The host made us sit back-to-back, and asked a series of questions about our relationship. We had to write down our answers on a piece of paper without saying anything to our partner, and share our answers at the end. The winners were the ones who had the most answers in common.

'Where did you meet your partner?'

That was an easy one. We both answered, 'At work.'

'Where was your first date?'

Another easy one. 'At the revolving restaurant at Sydney Tower.'

And then we came to some extremely embarrassing, agonisingly awkward questions.

'Where is the most interesting place you've had sex?'

It wasn't difficult to work that one out. 'On a cruise.' When the audience erupted into laughter, I explained, 'Well, we wanted to wait until we were married, so we haven't had an opportunity to try anywhere more interesting yet!' I heard a few *awwws* from the audience as my face turned a bright shade of red.

The host asked us, 'How many times have you been intimate on this cruise?'

I tried to count the number in my head, but in the end I had to make a guess. I answered 'eight' and Geoff answered 'nine', so we got that one wrong.

Because we answered more questions correctly than the other couples, we won a bottle of wine and a tacky golden statue in the shape of a Carnival cruise ship. We also received a thunderous round of applause from the crowd.

To my horror, the show had been recorded and was screened on repeat on the televisions in every single room for the remainder of the trip. I lost count of how many times strangers stopped us and said, 'Hey, you're that couple from the game show!' One guy shook Geoff's hand to congratulate him. 'Nice work, mate!'

CHAPTER 17

'Many are the plans in a person's heart, but it is
the LORD's purpose that prevails.'
—Proverbs 19:21 (NIV)

18 June – 12 September 2015

We conceived Charlie in our compact cabin on the cruise. The room didn't have any windows, so we were in total darkness when the lights were off. It was impossible to know what time of day it was, which meant we spent a lot of time in bed — not necessarily sleeping.

I suspected within a week that I was pregnant. My blood glucose levels had been constantly low, which isn't exactly normal when you're on a cruise stuffing your face with carbs all day long. I remembered reading somewhere that severe hypoglycaemia is common during early pregnancy in women with type 1 diabetes.

One night, after consuming enough pizza to feed a small village, I was startled to see my blood glucose had dropped to 0.8! It's a miracle that I didn't fall into a coma. My vision was blurry, and my lips were tingling. I thought it was strange, but initially I put it down to all the walking from one side of the ship to the other.

Upon returning home to Sydney, I peed on a pregnancy test before hopping into the shower. A few minutes later, I offhandedly asked Geoff through the shower screen, 'Are there two pink lines?'

'Yeah,' he said calmly, 'but one of them is really faint.'

'Cheekball! We're having a baby!'

The next day we went to see our GP, Dr Lee. In her strong Chinese accent, she asked me lots of questions, many of which we had to ask her to repeat because we couldn't understand what she was saying. She printed off a blood test referral, and we went straight to the pathologist to officially confirm the pregnancy.

When I returned to see Dr Lee a couple of days later, I was surprised when she told me, 'Blood test negative so maybe not pregnant. Or maybe did test too early.' She printed off a new referral, and we headed to the pathologist again.

I tried my best not to get my hopes up too high. I wondered, *Did I get a false positive on the home pregnancy test?* I Googled my question; it's apparently unlikely but it can happen. This time, however, the blood test confirmed that I was pregnant.

My pregnancy was considered 'high risk' due to my type 1 diabetes. This meant I couldn't book in to have the baby at either of my local hospitals in Manly or Mona Vale. So we made an appointment to see Dr Smith, an obstetrician and gynaecologist at Royal North Shore Hospital in St Leonards.

The drive was forty minutes from our home in Collaroy Plateau, and that was *without* traffic. But it was worth it; I knew immediately we were in safe hands. Dr Smith exuded warmth and compassion, making me feel truly cared for as he took his time to answer our questions.

I already knew that women with type 1 diabetes are advised not to try falling pregnant until their HbA1C is below 7.0 per cent, an indicator that their blood glucose levels have been mostly in target range for the previous three months. This is because poorly controlled type 1 diabetes brings with it additional risks, both for the baby (such as birth defects, miscarriage, and still birth) and for the mother (such as high blood pressure, eye damage, and having a large baby).

It's extremely challenging to maintain target blood glucose levels at the best of times, let alone during pregnancy. In the first trimester, I had hypos without much, if any, warning.

'Your body will be more sensitive to insulin, so you'll need smaller doses than you did before the pregnancy,' explained Dr Smith. 'But from the second trimester, your insulin requirements will start to increase.'

In the old days, doctors discouraged women with type 1 diabetes from getting pregnant at all. I'm so thankful that times have changed! Technology has improved so much, and there is a much better understanding of the effects of pregnancy on women with type 1 diabetes.

Although my HbA1C was already 'good enough' for pregnancy, my endocrinologist recommended that I switch from multiple daily insulin injections to an insulin pump so that I'd have even tighter blood glucose control.

An insulin pump is a battery-operated electronic device, smaller than the size of a mobile phone. A few people have asked me if it's a pager. *Um, no; it's not 1996*, I'd think to myself. It's worn twenty-four hours per day, and programmed to deliver insulin via thin plastic tubing known as an infusion set. A fine needle or flexible cannula is inserted just below the skin, and this stays in place for a few days before it needs to be replaced.

An insulin pump delivers small amounts of background insulin (or 'basal') continuously throughout the day, and allows me to give an extra dose of insulin (or 'bolus') whenever I eat carbohydrates, or to correct a high blood glucose level.

One advantage of using an insulin pump over injections is that the insulin is absorbed more efficiently and more predictably under the skin, resulting in fewer fluctuations in blood glucose levels, better flexibility in how much and when I can eat, and decreased risk of hypos during exercise.

My endocrinologist also recommended that I use a continuous glucose monitor. This is a device that automatically tracks your blood glucose levels, transmitting them via Bluetooth to the screen on your insulin pump every few minutes. Rather than multiple finger pricks per day, I can simply look at my insulin pump at any time and know exactly what my blood glucose level is. It lets me see whether my levels are trending low or high *before* they become dangerous.

I was both excited and nervous about the transition to an insulin pump and continuous glucose monitor. I'd been managing pretty well with injections, and I worried that making changes could potentially hurt the baby.

It was surreal to see our baby and to hear a heartbeat at the first ultrasound. It was slow, but the sonographer said that was normal because we were only five weeks pregnant at the time.

We'd already planned to have a second 'wedding reception' at our home for the friends and family we couldn't have at our actual wedding. We thought it would be perfect timing to share our good news then because I'd be thirteen weeks pregnant, so just into the second trimester.

The bleeding started on the twenty-ninth of August, two weeks before the party. Geoff wasn't home because he was working as an Uber driver at the time, so I phoned him.

'Can you please come home? I'm bleeding so much.'

I'm surprised he could understand what I was saying through my uncontrollable sobbing. He kicked his passenger out of his Micra and sped home.

Geoff drove me straight to the hospital. It was a few hours before a nurse saw me.

'Try not to stress,' she said. 'Bleeding in pregnancy can be perfectly normal.' I knew she was right. I'd seen reality television shows about women who didn't even know they were pregnant until they went into labour.

It was the middle of the night so I couldn't have an ultrasound at the hospital. Geoff and I went to a local imaging centre first thing the following morning. The floors rushed by as we stood in the elevator. I wanted time to stand still; I wasn't ready to hear that we'd lost the baby.

The sonographer's expression was serious as she performed the ultrasound.

'There's no heartbeat. It looks like the embryo stopped developing at six weeks.'

Embryo? I'd formed a deep connection with the baby the second I found out I was pregnant. It wasn't an 'embryo' growing inside me. He or she was a baby — *my* baby. The sonographer handed me a box of tissues to wipe the tears that rolled down my cheeks. I wondered how many women before me had pulled tissues from that same box.

I was admitted to hospital a few days later to have a dilatation and curettage, a surgical procedure where the cervix is dilated, and a special instrument is used to scrape the uterine lining. Dr Smith asked me to sign papers to confirm that I knew exactly what was about to happen to me. *Yes,*

I acknowledge that I'm about to have my baby taken away from me forever, I thought grimly as I ticked the box.

When I returned home just hours later, I went straight to bed, pulled the blanket up over my head, and wept. I felt profoundly empty.

To help cope with the grief, we gave the baby a name. I'd always loved the name 'Charlotte', but we settled on the unisex name 'Charlie' because it was too early to know if the baby was a boy or a girl.

We went ahead with the party. It should have been a time of celebration; instead, I was heartbroken. A friend who knew that we'd been expecting asked me, 'How are you feeling? Have you been getting any morning sickness?'

'No. We lost the baby,' I said, unable to hold back the tears. I quickly wiped them away, not wanting anyone else at the party to sense something was wrong.

I wondered, *Why did I just tell her I 'lost' the baby? It doesn't* feel *like I've lost Charlie*. Even now, our little one is never far from my thoughts.

'Oh, I'm so sorry,' my friend said. There are no magic words that can take the sorrow away from someone who has experienced a miscarriage. But simply being there for them and acknowledging that what they're going through sucks can make a difference.

It's extraordinary how much you can miss someone you've never met. From the moment I learned I was pregnant, I began to envision my future with Charlie. I didn't know what to do with my life now that he or she was no longer part of the picture. It wasn't just Charlie I'd lost; it was a piece of myself.

To our little Charlie

Two pink lines — we couldn't believe it was true;
We made phone calls to share the good news!
Would you wear pink, or would you wear blue?
Would you have your daddy's eyes? Would you have my nose?
Everyone was so excited to meet our little 'Peanut'.

But your days were like grass, flourishing like a flower of the field;
The wind passed over, and you were gone.
My world was ripped from beneath me that grim August night.
I prayed and prayed that the bleeding would stop;
That God wouldn't take you; that this was just a dream — a nightmare.

I cried in your daddy's arms when we hopped in the car;
Minutes turned into an eternity as we sat in the waiting room.
I wanted to hear that you were safe inside me,
But just after five o'clock, the nurse told us you were gone.
My heart raced. Yours had stopped.

They say you can't miss something you never had;
If that's true then why do I feel so sad?
So quickly you came into our lives, so quickly taken away.
You lived six short weeks, but we loved you so much.

The purpose of a life is God's to decide.
A man can live a thousand years but never find God and never know love.
A baby lost too soon can teach us about faith, and love, and draw us closer to
Him.
Yet still I ask, 'Why? Why couldn't I keep you?'
I wanted to give you everything — God gave you eternity.

We'll never know if you would wear pink or blue;
If you would have your daddy's eyes or my nose.
But I know we will meet you one day soon;
That you are safe in the arms of our loving Father,
And that is by far the safest place you could ever be.

CHAPTER 18

'Running an ultramarathon is 90 percent mental;
the other 10 percent — that's mental too.'
—Scott Jurek

BIG RED RUN
DAY 3

4 July 2014

I change into a fresh pair of black 2XU compression shorts, ready for our eight-thirty start time. Orange witch's hats line up beyond the start line to direct us out of camp. A flag with the Juvenile Diabetes Research Foundation logo waves in the gentle breeze, reminding me of one of the main reasons I'm out here — to prove to myself and others that having type 1 diabetes shouldn't stop you from achieving your goals.

I've raised close to $3,500 for the Juvenile Diabetes Research Foundation in the lead up to the race, and I've received more donations since arriving in Birdsville. My local newspaper, *Liverpool Leader*, even runs an article about me, stating, 'Running 150 kilometres in the middle of the Australian desert may not be everyone's cup of tea, but Stephanie is up to the challenge.' I know that running this ultramarathon will be worth every step if it means getting closer to finding a cure for the 130,000 Australians who live with type 1 diabetes.

I was first inspired to run long distances after reading the book, *Pole to Pole: One Man, 20 Million Steps* by legendary Australian endurance runner Pat Farmer. From April 2011 to January 2012, Pat ran an average of eighty kilometres per day to cover 21,000 kilometres between the North Pole and South Pole. He braved ice, jungle, and desert, raising over $100,000 for the Red Cross to build clean water wells.

Pat also holds the Guinness World Record for the fastest crossing of the Simpson Desert. In January 1998, with temperatures reaching fifty degrees Celsius, he ran the 379-kilometre traverse in just three days, eight hours, and thirty-six minutes!

As I climb over the Big Red sand dune for the last time, I say goodbye to the place I've called 'home' for the last two nights. The runners wave as the event helicopter swoops overhead. We must resemble tiny crawling ants to the pilot and photographers on board. I glance at all the footprints ahead of me, each one representing a person with their own unique story.

I quicken my pace when I make out a red tent on the horizon, signalling the first checkpoint at the eleven-kilometre mark. It's a pleasant surprise to see Dad waiting for me. I can only imagine how relieved he must be to see me, especially after my hypo on day one.

'Hey Dad! How's it going?'

'Yeah, not too bad,' he says. 'How are you? Do you need anything to eat?'

'No thanks, I'm okay. I'm not having a hypo right now, thankfully!'

Dad helps fill up my hydration flask. I'm sure this isn't the most exhilarating way to spend a morning, but he looks cheerful enough when I leave the checkpoint.

'Be careful!' Dad calls out after me.

'I will! See you soon.'

The dusty station tracks provide a welcome break from the difficult cross-country terrain of the desert. The ground is firm under my lime green and white HOKA trail shoes and easy to run on. It gives me a chance to switch off my brain because I don't need to concentrate too much on where I'm placing my feet.

I've been close on the heels of a fellow Little Red Runner for a few kilometres. Bill, a kind local council mayor from Kapunda, near the Barossa Valley in South Australia, maintains an impressive walking pace for someone in his sixties. With my head down, I zone out as I follow his footsteps.

I can just make out Bill in the distance and try my best to catch up to him. *You can do it. Just one foot in front of the other.* It's great to have a bit of friendly competition to motivate me to keep going. I'm finally within a hundred metres of Bill when I realise that I can't remember the last time I saw a pink flag.

Did Bill go the wrong way? He stops and turns around to face me, probably wondering the same thing. We retrace our steps together, searching high and low for a flag for the next ten minutes.

'Look! There it is!' I exclaim.

There's a rusty metal fence up ahead. *Did I go off track again?* I wonder. No; I can see pink flags on the other side of the fence. I can't climb over it, and I can't climb under it. If I want to get to the finish line, the only option is to climb *through* it. I do so, catching the flesh of my right thigh on a protruding wire in the process. *Ouch!*

Atop a wind-swept dune covered in emu and camel footprints, I gently pull apart the glued edges of Geoff's note for day three. I hear his voice in my head as I read his words:

During race day 3 — You're just amazing, you know that?

Geoff's note gives me the extra bit of encouragement I need to get to the finish line. After running the final stretch across gibber rocks, I'm greeted by cheers from the other Little Red Runners. I complete the 21.1 kilometres in a time of 3:12:49, placing fourth for the day.

I feel blessed to have made it this far. Many of the other runners, some of whom are experienced endurance athletes, have already been knocked down by injury. They're battling issues like Achilles tendinopathy, ankle sprains, and iliotibial band syndrome. It's miraculous that I don't have even a single blister at this stage of the race. Of course, there are still sixty-six kilometres left to run...

Our campsite for the next two nights sits on a gibber plain, enveloped by a sand dune amphitheatre. Innumerable stars emerge as the sun dips below the red dunes, painting the outback sky with changing hues of orange, purple, and pastel pink. I don't have words to describe the desert's grandeur that will do it any justice. It has a silent beauty that commands attention through its stillness.

Gazing up at the radiant glow of the Milky Way, I'm filled with awe and wonder at the vastness of the universe. It's humbling to contemplate that every single one of the two hundred billion trillion stars was handmade and hung in the sky by the Creator God.

I meditate on Psalm 8:3-4: 'When I look at your heavens, the work of your fingers, the moon and the stars, which you have set in place, what is man that you are mindful of him, and the son of man that you care for him?'

I'm overjoyed when I glimpse a wedge-tailed eagle soaring through the clouds high above me. I'm reminded of my all-time favourite verse in the Bible: 'But those who hope in the LORD will renew their strength. They will soar on wings like eagles; they will run and not grow weary, they will walk and not be faint' (Isaiah 40:31, NIV).

I believe this verse resonates so deeply with me because of my passion for running. I love its promise that though the troubles of life may fatigue us, God is an endless source of strength, generously giving it to all who place their hope in Him. And we don't have to *work* for it; we simply need to *wait* upon God.

CHAPTER 19

*'The steadfast love of the LORD never ceases; his mercies never come
to an end; they are new every morning; great is your faithfulness.'*
—Lamentations 3:22-23

December 2015 – January 2016

Soon after Christmas in 2015, I had an undeniable sense that new life was growing inside me. I've tried, and failed, to describe this feeling in words. There were no physical symptoms — no nausea, fatigue, or cramping. But I was certain that God was revealing it to me in my spirit.

I didn't think I would fall pregnant so soon after my miscarriage, but I bought a pregnancy test. I didn't tell Geoff, of course. He would have said it was a waste of money to take the test so early.

It wasn't; within a minute, two faint pink lines appeared on the stick. I was pregnant.

I pulled a single seed from a packet of chia seeds, and walked out to the balcony where Geoff was working at his makeshift 'stand-up desk' — an ironing board with a cardboard box sitting on top of it.

'Close your eyes and hold out your hand,' I said.

Geoff shut his eyes, and I placed the chia seed in his palm.

'Okay, open your eyes. This is how small our baby is right now,' I said. It only took a few seconds for him to understand what I was telling him. I felt such warmth as he wrapped me in his arms.

We went to see Dr Smith a couple of weeks later. He recommended that I stop running, at least during the first trimester. Although there are a multitude of positive effects associated with running during pregnancy, the relationship between running and miscarriage is somewhat unknown. It's possible that for those already at an increased risk of miscarriage, running could accelerate the process.

I wasn't willing to take the chance. I was determined to do everything in my power to protect our little 'CJ' (short for Cheekball Junior). So I accepted Dr Smith's advice without question and stopped running.

I also cut out my two favourite drinks, coffee and wine, from my diet. I was nowhere near as excited as I was when I was pregnant with Charlie. I was so fearful that something would go wrong. The last thing I wanted was a repeat of what we'd been through a few months earlier.

One night I had a terrifying nightmare. I was standing alone in our bathroom. A lake of crimson red blood surrounded me, and I fainted, collapsing onto the cold, hard tiles. My cries for Geoff went unanswered. The dream was so vivid that I woke up in a pool of sweat, my heart pounding out of my chest.

'What's the matter, Cheekball?' Geoff asked. I cuddled up to him, not saying a word, afraid that if I shared what I'd seen it would somehow come true.

At the six-week dating scan, we were thrilled to learn that the baby had a strong heartbeat. We prayed that CJ would be okay, and that God would keep our little one's tiny heart beating.

7 February 2016

I was baptised when I was seven weeks pregnant with CJ. Although I'd been a Christian for almost ten years, I hadn't yet taken the plunge. As Pastor Roy Barrett lowered me into the cool, murky waters of Manly Dam, I publicly declared my identity as a follower of Jesus Christ.

With jet skis roaring past in the distance, I reflected on my walk of faith over the previous decade. I could clearly see that God had been there with me on every step of the journey — through the struggles of living with type 1 diabetes; the self-doubt of taking my first steps into the world of running; the setback of my knee injury; the exceeding joy of finishing my first marathon; the heartache of my marriage breakdown; the good and not-so-good times in my relationship with Geoff; the tragedy of losing baby Charlie; the moments of *I want to live my life for you, God*; and the moments of *Just go away, God!*

I emerged from the water filled with an immense gratitude that God's love for me had never once wavered, and it never will. Nothing will ever be able to separate me from the love of God in Christ Jesus (Romans 8:38-39).

I take great comfort in knowing that He will continue to stay by my side — not because of anything I've done, for who am I? Through it all, God has been there. Through it all, He is there. Through it all, He will be there.

8 – 15 February 2016

The bleeding started the next day. Instead of rejoicing in my baptism, I was overcome with sadness. This time, though, I felt God's presence amid the tears. I put my trust in God in the circumstances. *Not my will, but Yours,*

Lord, I prayed. I experienced a peace I'd never known before, and unwavering confidence in God and His plan for my life.

Dr Smith fit us into his busy schedule the following morning. He immediately set me up for an ultrasound in his room.

'This machine isn't very advanced and can't always pick up the baby's heartbeat,' he said, sliding the cold, gooey gel over my abdomen. 'I'll get you to head down the hall to the ultrasound theatre to check that the baby is okay.'

Geoff and I sat hand-in-hand in the waiting room. I prayed that this was all just a nightmare, like the one I'd had about bleeding in our bathroom. The sonographer called us in, and I held my breath as she pushed the probe over my abdomen. After what felt like an eternity, she said, 'I'm so sorry. The baby's heart isn't beating.'

Dr Smith booked me in to have my second dilatation and curettage surgery on the fifteenth of February. By that stage I was in the worst physical agony I'd ever been in. It was like a knife repeatedly stabbing me in the abdomen. I was losing so much blood and passing large clots.

Geoff did his best to comfort me each time I emerged from the bathroom, sobbing after seeing what I assumed were pieces of our dead baby. It felt like life was draining out of me. I had no strength to do anything except lay in bed, curled up in fetal position, waiting to go to the hospital for the procedure.

CHAPTER 20

'Would you tell me, please, which way I ought to go from here?'
'That depends a good deal on where you want to get to,' said the Cat.
'I don't much care where —' said Alice.
'Then it doesn't matter which way you go,' said the Cat.
'— so long as I get somewhere,*' Alice added as an explanation.*
'Oh, you're sure to do that,' said the Cat, 'if only you walk long enough.'
—Lewis Carroll

16 – 17 December 2015

We established our status as amateur hikers when we set off on our adventure with cans of beer in our hands. Geoff and I make the most of every opportunity to go bushwalking with our friend Rob. This time, like every time before, we were in search of a challenge.

Of all the walks we could have chosen in the Blue Mountains, of course we picked one recommended for 'experienced walkers only'. At sixteen kilometres return, the distance between the Golden Staircase and Chinamans Gully (via Mount Solitary and Ruined Castle) isn't particularly long. However, with a total elevation of 1,048 metres, it would be no mean feat.

We were disorganised from the get-go. We didn't even check the weather forecast until we were on the way and saw a storm brewing on the horizon. It was a miracle that we remembered to pack our rain jackets. It wasn't until we arrived in Katoomba, ninety minutes' drive west of Sydney, that Rob realised he'd forgotten to bring his sleeping bag. We had to wait for a camping store to open at nine before we could even begin the hike.

I'm not too sure what we were thinking when we decided we didn't need to pack a tent. I'd read online that there was a cave at the campsite at Chinamans Gully, but we had no idea what the cave would be like. What if it didn't offer us the protection we needed, especially if it were to rain?

I think the only thing we planned thoroughly was our food supply, with a decent portion of time spent making sure we had the right quantity of orange juice for our vodka.

🏃 🏃 🏃

Geoff parked his Micra in a secluded spot at the foot of the track.

'It's a bit creepy here,' I whispered as we unloaded the boot. Geoff would be carrying the bulk of our gear because his backpack was much bigger than mine and Rob's.

'Rob-ball!' Geoff exclaimed, using our nickname for Rob. Geoff was grumpy with Rob for getting dirt in the car because, as an Uber driver, he took pride in keeping it spotless (if only that was still the case!).

'Um, Cheekball,' I said, 'we're about to go on an overnight hike. You do realise the car is going to need a good clean after we get back into it tomorrow, right?'

We cracked open our beers, snapped a selfie, and hit the trail. We started with an eight hundred-metre descent down the steep metal and wooden steps of the Golden Staircase. It wasn't long before a rainstorm rolled in, making the eroded path slippery. When I mentioned earlier that we all had rain jackets, I didn't say anything about their quality. Geoff's was more like a poncho and incredibly impractical. His clothes were soaked through within minutes.

'Should we keep going?' asked Rob, stroking his full ginger beard. 'Maybe we should turn back. What if it rains like this the entire way?'

We considered heading back to the car and booking a hostel for the night. Instead, we pushed on, agreeing that if any of us wanted to turn back at any time then we'd do so together as a team.

The track flattened out into a wide trail through a lush green rainforest filled with fern trees and vines. We soon heard the song of a lyrebird echoing around the valley.

'Oh, wow! Check it out, guys!' I whispered, motioning to the lyrebird strutting across the track ahead of us.

The vibrant red of the native waratah plant, the floral emblem of New South Wales, was in abundance at the base of Ruined Castle, a rock formation jutting out of the Jamison Valley. I noticed a sign and read the words aloud to Geoff and Rob:

WARNING
Remote area
Indistinct route
Steep terrain
Exposed climbing
Loose surfaces
No reliable water
Carry plenty

The final two words on this sign must have somehow slipped our collective memory by the time we finished the steep climb up Ruined Castle. To lighten our load, we stashed a few bottles of water between a couple of rocks. We figured we wouldn't need them until our return walk the following day, so there was no point in carrying them the entire way.

After a quick break enjoying a 360-degree panorama of the Jamison Valley from Katoomba to Leura, we set off on what would prove to be the most challenging section of the hike. There was a steep descent for a few hundred metres on a path covered with loose soil, and the wet weather had turned it into a natural slip and slide.

At the bottom, Rob sheepishly said, 'Um, guys… I've split my shorts.'

Geoff and I burst out laughing, seeing a great deal more humour in the situation than Rob did.

Next, we had an extremely steep scramble to the top of Mount Solitary. Geoff, a naturally gifted climber, was always way ahead of Rob and me. We never lost sight of him, though, because he wore the same hideous board shorts he'd proposed to me in.

While Rob and I struggled to clamber up the Korrowall Knife Edge, Geoff was his usual daredevil self, easily scaling giant boulders that didn't look at all safe. At one point we had to squeeze ourselves between a narrow gap in a three-metre-tall rock wall. Oh, did I mention that Rob is terrified of heights?

The pouring rain made the hike so much more difficult than we were prepared for. There weren't many markers to show us which direction to walk, and at one point we weren't sure if we'd be able to continue. I guarantee we were all thinking the same thing as we sat crammed together and shivering in a little cave: *This is miserable.*

With barely any space to sit comfortably, we evaluated the situation over a lunch of tuna and salad wraps. We christened the cave 'The Cave of Despair'. But when the rain clouds began to disperse, unveiling spectacular views out to the surrounding Blue Mountains, we renamed it 'The Cave of Hope'.

We were exhausted when we finally arrived at the sandstone plateau at the top of Mount Solitary. To be honest, the scenery didn't exactly blow me away. Perhaps I was too weary to appreciate it? In any case, I was glad that we'd made it to the summit with no casualties — except for Rob's shorts, that is.

The track wound downhill for another kilometre or so, before arriving at a flat clearing with a large rock wall nestled beside a small creek. I couldn't believe it — we'd finally made it to the campsite at Chinamans Gully. But where was the promised cave I'd read about? It turns out the 'cave' was simply a slight overhang of the rock wall. Oh well. At least we'd be somewhat sheltered from the elements.

Geoff was the hero of the day, building an impressive fire that he managed to keep going the entire night. We huddled together around the flames as Rob entertained us with his animated hand gestures and ceaseless stream of words. We roasted marshmallows and sipped plastic cups filled with the perfect ratio of vodka to orange juice. We all agreed that it had been a good move not to turn back when things got tough at the Cave of Despair/Hope.

We did it all again the next day. We were on the verge of running out of water when we arrived back at Ruined Castle. We should have taken the advice on that sign because we couldn't find our water bottles anywhere!

'Are you one hundred per cent sure this is where we left them?' I asked Geoff.

'Yep, I'm sure. Someone must have taken them.'

The final climb up the Golden Staircase was brutal, especially because we were all a little dehydrated. But the backdrop of mist-covered mountains made it worth the effort. We ended the hike in much the same way as we'd begun, by celebrating with a couple of beers at the local pub.

'So, where to next, team?'

CHAPTER 21

'Some seek the comfort of their therapist's office, others head to the corner pub and dive into a pint, but I chose running as my therapy.'
—Dean Karnazes

February – October 2016

I fell into a deep darkness in the wake of my miscarriages.

'I'm so angry that God allowed this to happen!' I confided in Geoff. 'Doesn't God love me? Is He punishing me for something?'

I couldn't understand why these tragedies had occurred. It didn't seem fair. I screamed out to God; I don't know what I wanted from Him, but I was hurting and needed Him to know.

We didn't have funerals for Charlie and CJ. I wonder sometimes whether having them might have helped with the grieving process. I know my babies are in Heaven, but where are their earthly bodies? Did the nurses dump their remains in a surgical bin? Were they cremated? I regret not asking for their bodies so I could bury them.

My throat tightened whenever I walked past the baby section in Kmart, with the soft pastel onesies and tiny shoes a painful reminder of what I'd lost. I rejected an invitation to my friend's baby shower. I scrolled past my friends' pregnancy announcements on Facebook without clicking 'Like' or leaving a comment to congratulate them. I know they were just going about their lives; they weren't doing anything to intentionally upset me. But I found it impossible to share in their joy because I wanted so desperately to be in their place.

Mother's Day came around, bringing another surge of heartache for the children I would never hold in my arms. Although they were only inside me for a fleeting moment, I became a mother the instant I conceived my first child. The love I have for them has been unaffected by the passage of time.

I wanted a baby more than anything else in the world. I didn't know what to say when friends would ask, 'So when are you having kids?' It wasn't long before the question became, 'Why haven't you had kids yet?' They didn't realise how much pain was attached to these questions, of course. The silent sadness of miscarriage often goes unseen.

I don't know the reason for my miscarriages. When I lost CJ, I blamed myself. I worried that I'd eaten the wrong foods, or pushed myself too hard at the gym, or hadn't done enough to keep my blood glucose levels stable.

'It's not your fault,' Dr Smith said. 'You haven't done anything wrong, so please don't be hard on yourself.'

But I couldn't help it. I was haunted by the thought that Charlie and CJ had suffered when they died.

Friends who knew about our struggles tried to comfort me with statements like, 'Miscarriage is common; it happened to a friend of mine,' or 'Don't worry. You're still young. You have plenty of time to try again.' Their words felt dismissive, as if my grief didn't matter. It's true that one in four pregnancies ends in miscarriage, but statistics do little to ease the pain of loss.

One of my Christian friends did her best to encourage me by saying, 'You just need to have more faith! Maybe try praying like Hannah did in the Bible.' 1 Samuel 1-2 tells the story of Hannah, a barren woman who persistently cried out to God to bless her with a son. God eventually answered her prayers with the birth of Samuel. My friend's well-meaning comments only made me feel more at fault. I was ashamed that I didn't have 'enough' faith.

I also felt fatigued and bloated, and I'd drink alcohol when I was home alone — not to get drunk, but to numb the pain. It didn't work, of course; it made me more depressed. I knew I wouldn't survive if something didn't change. Drawing upon God's strength, I laced up my running shoes and headed out the front door.

🏃🏃🏃

My first run after the miscarriage was a short loop around Long Reef headland. Although I'd been doing strength classes a couple of times per week at the gym, I'd lost so much cardiovascular fitness. I was beyond exhausted at the end of the run, but I was glad to have something positive to keep my mind occupied.

At first, I wondered if I was attempting to run away from my grief. If so, it didn't work because I only experienced a temporary sense of comfort. I'd return home after each run, and the sadness would still be there. I realised that rather than running *away* from the grief, I was running *through* it.

As the months went by, running helped to shift my mindset. I'd been so focused on my body as something that was broken, and on what it wasn't able to achieve. But the action of running gave me a sense of awe for what my body *could* achieve.

Running gave me the headspace to process my grief. It reminded me that despite my loss, there was still so much good in the world. Rather than dwelling on the things I *didn't* have, I began to appreciate the things that God had already blessed me with.

I was grateful for the simple things in life — the exhilaration of running in the rain, the beauty of an early morning sunrise, and the 'good' kind of sore when you know you've pushed your body to its absolute physical limits.

As I gradually built my fitness back up, I enjoyed going on adventures again. Geoff and I went on hikes with friends, including a thirty-five-kilometre walk along the coast from Manly to Palm Beach, a sixteen-kilometre stroll through Garigal National Park, and a twenty-six-kilometre overnight trek between Bundeena and Otford in southern Sydney's Royal National Park.

I also made a successful return to trail racing, completing the shorter distances at the Sydney Trail Series (the first in Botany Bay, and the second and third at Manly Dam). I won the overall series in my age category!

Okay, technically I won by default since I was the only female aged between twenty and twenty-nine to complete all three events. But despite wrestling with imposter syndrome, hearing my name announced as the winner made my day. I proudly accepted my prize — a brand-new pair of running shorts — grateful for how far I'd come over the past nine months.

CHAPTER 22

*'Only those who will risk going too far can
possibly find out how far they can go.'*
—T.S. Eliot

23 – 27 April 2016

In April 2016, I experienced grief for the third time in two years. I was
volunteering at a checkpoint for the Anzac Day Challenge in Ku-ring-gai
Chase National Park (the lucky participants didn't have to run 155 laps of
an oval like I did two years earlier!).

I heard my phone ringing and saw the name *Dad* on the screen. We usually send text messages rather than speaking on the phone, so I immediately
knew that something must be wrong.

His voice quivered as he spoke the words: 'Yiayia's in hospital. The doctors have said she doesn't have long to live.'

I hung up, tears streaming down my face. I didn't care that the other
volunteers were staring at me, wondering what on earth I was so upset
about. We were still setting up the checkpoint and the race hadn't even
started yet, but I knew I had to get to the hospital. A fellow volunteer had
given me a lift to the checkpoint because the trail was only accessible by
four-wheel drive, and he kindly offered to give me a lift back to my car.

When I reached the hospital, Yiayia was already unconscious. She'd been battling with emphysema for many years. Mum and Uncle Jim stood at her bedside, holding each of her hands in theirs. I was distressed to see Yiayia like that. Under the white sheet was not the energetic, vibrant grandmother I'd always looked up to, but a frail, lifeless body. Her lungs fought desperately for oxygen. There was a pause after every breath, with each one stretching longer and longer. Four days later, she drew her final breath.

October 2016

I applied to join the Australian Defence Force's Army Reserve in October 2016. It was something I'd wanted to do for a decade. In fact, I'd first made an application in 2006, but I'd been forced to cancel it due to my knee injury.

Why did I want to do it? Was I trying to prove myself? Maybe... but to whom? I wasn't really sure. One thing I do know is that I love stepping out of my comfort zone.

I trained for the Pre-entry Fitness Assessment for several months. I ran three or four days per week because I needed to achieve a beep test score of 7.5 to be accepted. The beep test is pure torture. It involves running back and forth between two lines that are twenty metres apart. You need to reach each line before you hear the *beep*; if not, you're out. The challenge is that the time between each beep gets shorter and shorter.

One afternoon, Geoff and I went down to a local soccer field to practice. We used Geoff's running shoes to mark out the lines (he prefers running barefoot anyway), and I pressed start on a recording of the beep test on the Australian Defence Force app.

My lungs burned as each beep drew closer and closer. I only reached 6.8 on my first attempt, so I had a fair bit of work to do. I knew I had the physical fitness to achieve a 7.5, but I also had post-traumatic stress disorder from being one of the first kids to drop out whenever we did the beep test in high school. So it would come down to a battle of mind versus body.

Geoff and I worked out a couple of times per week at Queenscliff Beach with our friend and qualified personal trainer Gary. In return for a full-body workout, we'd buy Gary a big breakfast of eggs Benedict with smoked salmon at a local beachside café.

Gary's sessions were gruelling, and no two were the same. He took us through drills involving push-ups, lunges, squats, burpees, bicycle crunches, planks, stair climbs, swimming, crab crawls, bear crawls, kettlebell swings, and every other exercise you can possibly think of.

Normally full of jokes, Gary would be so serious during the hour, not letting us slacken off for a second. Geoff and I rarely felt like going, but there was always a sense of accomplishment afterwards, especially knowing that we'd made it to the end without dying.

I was steadily building up my upper body and core strength. I had to be able to do eight push-ups to qualify for the Army Reserve. That probably doesn't sound like many to most people, but I've always sucked at proper push-ups. I'd only ever been able to do 'girl push-ups', where you're propped up on your knees rather than your toes. I started out barely able to do two with the correct technique; I was so proud of myself when I could finally do eight!

However, after all the hard work I'd put in, my application was rejected. The Australian Defence Force has a blanket ban placed on anyone with type 1 diabetes. This was despite my endocrinologist writing them a letter to confirm that I was medically suitable, and that my type 1 diabetes would have no impact on my obligations within the Australian Defence Force.

I was so disappointed and wrote the following email in response to the decision:

To whom it may concern,

I am writing to appeal the decision made regarding my medical suitability for military service. I believe having type 1 diabetes shouldn't exclude me from selection.

My diabetes is incredibly well-controlled. In fact, my diabetes educator told me last week that it's as though I don't have diabetes at all! My most recent HbA1C in September was 5.8%, and I wear a continuous glucose monitor that lets me know what my blood glucose levels are at all times.

I would very much appreciate the opportunity to continue the recruitment process. Thank you for your time and consideration.

Kind regards,
Stephanie Walters

My email had no impact whatsoever on their decision. This wasn't the first time that type 1 diabetes had been a barrier to me pursuing a career I really wanted. When I was in primary school, I had to do a school assignment on aeroplanes. I drew a picture of a plane on one of those giant sheets of coloured cardboard, and carefully labelled all its distinct parts. Although I'd never been on a plane before, I became fascinated by them and decided that I wanted to become a pilot when I grew up. When I told Mum about my dream, she said, 'You can't be a pilot if you have diabetes, bub.' I was heartbroken.

What I wouldn't give to live twenty-four hours without type 1 diabetes! To eat whatever I want, whenever I want, without having to work out how much insulin to give myself. To go out for a run at any time without needing to take a snack with me in case I have a hypo. To not base my shopping decisions on whether an item of clothing has a pocket for my insulin pump. To sleep through the night without being woken by the buzz of my continuous glucose monitor. To enjoy a dip in the ocean, rather than worrying that I've been disconnected from my insulin pump for too long.

Still, I try my best to live by a 'No Excuses' philosophy. I've learned over the years that thinking of myself as a 'type 1 diabetic runner' can be harmful. Instead, I remind myself that I'm a runner who also happens to have type 1 diabetes. I am so much more than my autoimmune condition, so I don't ever want to let it define me.

CHAPTER 23

'Alone we can do so little; together we can do so much.'
—Helen Keller

14 June – 5 July 2016

I returned to Birdsville in 2016, this time as a volunteer for the Big Red Run with Geoff. Instead of taking the most direct route (north-west from Sydney as Dad and I had done), we chose a much longer journey via Wagga Wagga in New South Wales, Mildura in Victoria, and Marree in South Australia. We'd need to travel approximately 2,500 kilometres to reach Birdsville.

We kicked off our adventure in the harbourside eastern Sydney suburb of Watsons Bay. This is where we *should* have spent our wedding night. Instead, Geoff's frugal side had kicked into overdrive, and he booked a shabby three-star hotel in Potts Point through the accommodation website *Wotif.*

I can still recall my disappointment when I entered the room, and discovered there was barely enough space to move around it in my wedding dress. In Geoff's defence, he genuinely believed he'd secured a great deal for a luxury hotel.

Geoff made things right by booking a room for our one-year anniversary at Watsons Bay Boutique Hotel. I had my wedding dress altered into a midi-length dress to mark the occasion, and we celebrated in style on the waterfront with a glass or three of champagne.

The next morning, we set off on our road trip to the centre of Australia. We needed a four-wheel drive because it was unlikely that Geoff's Micra or my Mirage would successfully make it to Birdsville. So we bought a forest green 2000 Mitsubishi Pajero from a man named Jesus for the bargain price of $1,600 (we later sold it for about $4,000!). It was such a blessing from God.

That said, the Green Beast didn't even survive the two-hour drive to Bowral before we heard a loud *pop* coming from the engine.

'What was that?!' I exclaimed.

Geoff slowed to a stop on the side of the Hume Motorway. A hose had come loose, so we had to organise a tow truck to get it to a mechanic in the next town. We were back on the road again within a couple of hours.

Dad had spent hours building a bed frame in the back of the Green Beast, with four storage compartments underneath to stash all our gear. A true do-it-yourself enthusiast, Dad effortlessly brought our vision to life by designing a compact home on wheels. We hung beach towels over the windows each night, serving as makeshift curtains that created a cosy cocoon of privacy.

🏃 🏃 🏃

I loved playing tour guide to Geoff as we drove around Wagga Wagga. I pointed out all the places I visited during my time there as a university student between 2006 and 2010.

'So, this is Wagga Beach,' I informed Geoff as we wandered along the shore of the Murrumbidgee River. 'I used to float down the river and have picnics here with my friends.'

'Um, this isn't a beach, Cheekball.'

I laughed. 'Yep, I agree. The whole time I lived here, I never understood why it was called a 'beach'. I mean it's literally a riverbank, hundreds of kilometres from the coast.'

After spending a week sleeping in the back of the Green Beast, I was keen to enjoy a couple of nights in a proper bed. We were Groupon enthusiasts at the time, and I found an irresistible deal for a 'glamping' experience at Wilpena Pound in the Ikara-Flinders Ranges National Park of South Australia. Located five hours north of Adelaide, Wilpena Pound is a natural amphitheatre of mountains, renowned for its rich geological history, ancient fossils, and remarkable Aboriginal rock art.

'Can we *please* go, Cheekball?'

It took a bit of convincing, but Geoff soon agreed to the unforeseen holiday expense. Glamping means staying in a tent but with the added luxury of a bar fridge, air conditioning, toilet, shower, king size bed, and coffee making facilities.

Geoff and I relaxed in our tent with a delicious bottle of red wine we'd purchased the day before from the Clare Valley, Australia's oldest wine region. We shared another bottle as we took a stroll to watch the moon climb into the sky. Heavenly lights soon shone above us, without a single artificial light to compete with.

We enjoyed our time alone together in the countryside. Let's just say that if the game show host from the cruise had another chance to ask us about the most interesting place we'd done the deed, our answer would have been different.

We rose early the next morning to climb to the top of St Mary Peak, or Ngarri Mudlanha in the local language. At 1,189 metres, St Mary Peak is the highest mountain in the Flinders Ranges. It was a demanding nineteen-kilometre trek, so I was devastated when we weren't rewarded with

Google's promise of 'panoramic views' when we reached the summit. In fact, we couldn't see *anything* through the thick white fog enveloping the mountain!

Fortunately, by the time we'd finished eating our packed lunch, the fog had cleared enough to reveal a 360-degree vista of rolling green hills and vast salt plains.

Our next stop was Marree, a small outback town located three and a half hours from Wilpena Pound in the north-east of South Australia. This was the first time on our road trip where I felt like we were truly in the desert. We glimpsed herds of wild brown horses galloping over extremely barren and isolated plains.

We camped overnight in a caravan park, where we enjoyed mingling with a group of German tourists around a crackling campfire.

'Ve haf been schtrented here fur a veek. Ve do nicht haf a four-veel drife undt ze Birtsfille Track iss nicht open to two-veel drifes.'

I translated this to mean, 'We've been stranded here for a week. We don't have a four-wheel drive, and the Birdsville Track isn't open to two-wheel drives.'

The Birdsville Track is a famous 517-kilometre outback road stretching between Marree and Birdsville, traversing the Strzelecki, Sturt Stony, and Tirari Deserts. Recent above average rainfall in the region had made the Birdsville Track unsuitable for some vehicles.

Later, out of earshot of the Germans, I said to Geoff, 'Oh man, I'm so glad we bought the Green Beast!'

We stopped at the Mungerannie Hotel, a rustic homestead with a history dating back to 1886. Roughly halfway between Marree and Birdsville, it's the only fuel stop on the Birdsville Track.

The owner Phil, with his scruffy beard and well-worn Akubra hat, greeted us with a big grin. Phil was sociable, with a quirky character and quick wit. He was already unapologetically drunk by the time we arrived at eleven in the morning.

The pub's ceiling was covered in all kinds of strange paraphernalia, including snippets of human hair, hats, rusty signs, flags, stubby coolers, and five-dollar notes, all sourced from past guests who'd enjoyed a beverage there.

'Would you like a drink?' Phil asked.

'Oh, no thanks. We've got to get going to Birdsville soon,' Geoff replied.

'No charge, mate.' We found ourselves sipping beer and vodka out the front of the pub with Phil. This is where I first met my beautiful friend Anja. We formed an instant bond when I noticed the insulin pump clipped to her hip pocket.

'So, what brings you to the middle of nowhere?' I asked.

'I'm a nurse and I'm volunteering on the medical team at an ultramarathon in Birdsville,' she replied.

'No way! We're volunteers there too! What a small world.'

I've made so many friends within the type 1 diabetes community over the years, both on social media and at different events. I feel a sense of belonging with them because they understand what it's like to have type 1 diabetes — the effort that goes into counting carbs, the frustration when your continuous glucose monitor chart looks more like a roller coaster than a straight line, and the financial burden that comes with buying everything we need to survive. There's something comforting in knowing that I'm not alone, and that there are others out there who not only live but thrive with type 1 diabetes.

By early afternoon, Phil was far too incapacitated to serve drinks. He disappeared without a word, likely to sleep off the effects of all the beer he'd consumed. Us patrons were left to fend for ourselves.

A heavyset man took over the running of the bar, amusing us with tales of his four-wheel driving adventures through the Simpson Desert. He charged five dollars for every drink or snack, regardless of its actual value.

I scratched my head as we drove away from Mungerannie Hotel the following morning, trying to work out if what we'd experienced there was real or just a dream.

We spotted a bus stop with a sign towering above it that said, *McDonald's Opening Soon*. I was craving a Big Mac, but we were 580 kilometres from the closest Macca's. I couldn't resist taking a photo of this bizarre example of classic outback humour.

After ten days on the road, Geoff and I finally made it to Birdsville. Volunteering at the Big Red Run gave me a newfound appreciation for the incredible human beings who give up so much of their time and energy to help at races. I learned a valuable lesson in the importance of giving back to the running community. Without the generosity of volunteers, events simply cannot go ahead.

There was a downpour of rain on day one of the race. A thick layer of oozing orange-brown mud engulfed the first campsite. We sunk deeper and deeper into it with every step we took until it came up to our ankles. Our shoes grew heavier and heavier as more and more mud caked itself onto them.

If I had to use a Portaloo, I'd put it off as long as possible before making the effort to trudge through the mud. The volunteers used shovels to clear the mud, forming a dirt path between the food tent, runners' tents, and Portaloos.

The runners were exhausted after completing an entire marathon that day; I couldn't imagine walking, let alone running, that far in these conditions. The event organisers made the tough decision to cancel the second day of the race. I'm sure this must have been disappointing for the runners after the hours of training they'd put in.

Despite this, laughter erupted as we watched each other slip and slide on the rest day. We were all amused when Ed Sheeran's soulful tune 'Thinking Out Loud' blared over the campsite:

When your legs don't work like they used to before…

Geoff and I were responsible for marking out the course for the runners. Wearing our daggy fly hats, we carefully followed a map on a tablet so we knew exactly where to stick the pink flags in the ground or hang pink ribbons on trees and shrubs. Experience had taught me how crucial it was to do our job well; if we placed the markers too far apart, the runners would inevitably get lost.

I was awestruck by the stark contrast between what the desert looked like in 2016 compared to 2014. It was so much greener! A carpet of white, yellow, and purple wildflowers covered the slopes of the sand dunes. The salt lakes, usually hard and firm, were soft and boggy, filled with flood waters from the recent rain.

Even though we had a four-wheel drive, Geoff and I still managed to get bogged. We were driving out to a checkpoint on the final day when we reached a section of road that was flooded over.

Luckily, a Good Samaritan pulled his car alongside ours.

'G'day! Looks like you folks are a bit stuck. Can I give you a hand?' He waded waist deep into the murky water to help us free the Green Beast.

I was thankful we'd decided against driving the Micra. For one thing, we wouldn't have been able to get far in a two-wheel drive; for another, Geoff would never have been able to do Uber driving in it again. Every inch of the Green Beast, both inside and out, was coated in mud. Weeks later, back home in Sydney, we were still scrubbing dirt off it.

CHAPTER 24

*'Our achievements are generally limited only by
the beliefs we impose on ourselves.'*
—Bear Grylls

14 November 2016 – 27 January 2017

In late 2016, I set myself a formidable goal to run non-stop up the infamous Alexander Street in Collaroy. This 250-metre behemoth of a hill is the sixth steepest in Sydney, with a respectable 21.7 per cent gradient. For someone who has always dreaded hills, the challenge was on par with conquering Mount Everest.

I knew it would be more of a mental hurdle for me than a physical one. My first attempt took place on the fourteenth of November 2016. I made my way up at a sluggish pace of nine minutes and seventeen seconds per kilometre. Feelings of self-doubt crept in within the first hundred metres. *What were you thinking, Steph? You can't do this. Just give up.* My lungs were on fire, my heart was bursting out of my chest, my calves were burning up, salty sweat stung my eyes, and I surrendered to my negative thoughts and stopped running.

My second attempt wasn't until the twenty-seventh of January 2017. I'd put in weeks of training involving brutal hill repetitions and stair sprints. This time my pace was much faster at eight minutes and forty seconds per kilometre. I felt the curious gazes of onlookers from their front porch. They must have thought I was nuts. But I didn't care. *It doesn't matter how fast or slow you move*, I told myself. *Just keep moving. You can do it, Steph.* And I did! I conquered Alexander Street!

I've discovered that the trick with climbing hills is to take them one small step at a time. Rather than fixating on how far you still have to go, concentrate on making short, steady strides, even if it feels like you're moving at a snail's pace.

Like a steep hill, the challenges of life can often seem insurmountable. The path is anything but smooth, filled with obstacles and unexpected twists and turns. It's natural to feel disheartened when progress seems painfully slow.

My advice? Enjoy the journey! Resist the urge to glance too far ahead; instead, focus on running the kilometre you're in. Each step builds strength and resilience as you move closer to your goal. Before you know it, you'll reach the top and be able to look back and truly appreciate just how far you've come!

4 – 26 February 2017

I kicked off the 2017 race season with the Sun Run. The hilly course stretches for seven kilometres between Dee Why and Manly, taking in the impressive coastline of Sydney's northern beaches along the way. It was handy having a race that started less than ten minutes' drive from our front door.

I record all my race results on an Excel spreadsheet — I blame my accountant husband for that! — and I've never run a faster pace in a race. I managed to conquer the three hills with an average pace of five minutes and ten seconds per kilometre, putting me in the top nine per cent of all participants, and the top three per cent in both my age and gender categories. I looked forward to seeing what else the year had in store for me.

In 2016, after completing a Postgraduate Certificate in Editing and Electronic Publishing at Macquarie University, I eagerly set up my own proofreading and copyediting business, Comma Sense Editing. I couldn't think of a more rewarding career than being a book editor, having loved reading since I was a little girl.

On Valentine's Day 2017, I started a part-time role as an Administration Assistant at a friend's insurance business in Surry Hills. This job helped to supplement my income while I focused on building my editing business.

Just one week into the job, I vaguely recall sitting at my desk and scratching an itch on the side of my left thigh. I discreetly pulled up my skirt to see a tiny speck of blood, but the sore seemed so insignificant that I didn't think anything of it.

A few days later, wanting to avoid travelling home from work in peak hour traffic, Geoff and I drove to Centennial Park to go for a jog. We'd planned to run two or three loops, but I only needed to take a few steps to realise that maybe this wasn't going to be possible. I could barely walk, let alone run. The pain in my left thigh was excruciating! It was crazy to think that something so small could cause so much agony.

Geoff's eyebrows drew together when he saw my face grimacing with each step.

'Are you okay, Cheekball?' he asked.

'Yeah, I'm okay. I'll push through.' I tried to hide how I was feeling with a smile, but I knew it showed. I'd never give up my day job to become an actor.

'Okay, just see how you go. If it hurts too much, we'll turn back.'

We barely made it three hundred metres before the pain became unbearable.

'I'm sorry; I have to stop.'

I examined my thigh thoroughly as we drove home. The flesh around the sore was bright red and a small lump had formed. Freaking out because Doctor Google told me a spider had bitten me, I asked Geoff, 'Can you drive me to the hospital?'

Sitting in the waiting room, I re-read my favourite Charles Dickens novel, *A Christmas Carol*, to pass the time. But it was difficult to focus on dear Tiny Tim when all I could think was that I might die from this or, worse, have my leg amputated.

'Stephanie Walters?' called out a nurse from behind a clipboard.

I explained my concerns when I sat down with her. 'I think I might have been bitten by a spider.'

'It was probably just a harmless insect, but it does look infected,' she said, marking a circle around the sore with a black pen. 'I'm sure it'll be fine. Just take these antibiotics tonight and tomorrow morning, and come back if the redness has spread outside the circle.'

The next day saw no improvement. The redness had spread well outside the circle the nurse had drawn. I went back to the emergency room late that night and was admitted straight away. A different antibiotic was pumped into a vein in my right arm.

Although I was scared and wanted Geoff to stay with me, I told him, 'You go home and get a good night's sleep.' I couldn't do the same; behind the curtain in the bed next to mine, a man spent the night yelling at the nurses. He was obviously under the influence of alcohol or some other drug. I don't think I got more than a couple of hours' sleep that night.

CHAPTER 25

'For our light and momentary troubles are achieving for us an eternal glory that far outweighs them all. So we fix our eyes not on what is seen, but on what is unseen, since what is seen is temporary, but what is unseen is eternal.'
—2 Corinthians 4:17-18 (NIV)

27 February – 22 March 2017

I was sound asleep when Geoff arrived at the hospital early the next morning.

'How are you feeling?' he asked.

'Pretty rubbish. I need to get out of this place.'

I'd gone from running long distances to struggling to walk two metres to the bathroom. Not to mention I was feeling guilty about taking sick leave from my new job so soon after I'd started.

'Here are your discharge papers,' said a nurse, placing paperwork on my cluttered food tray. 'The doctor will be in to see you, but you should be good to go very soon!'

I hesitated, wanting to leave the hospital so badly, yet sure that my leg wasn't any better.

'Um, I think it's getting worse,' I said.

'Oh, do you mind if I have a look?' She pulled the crisp, white hospital sheet down around my leg. I had a giant lump on my thigh. It was red raw and felt warm to touch.

'Hmmm…' she said.

When the doctor arrived, he took one look at my leg and said, 'We'll have to operate to drain the abscess.' He explained that an abscess is a confined collection of pus surrounded by inflamed tissue. It forms when bacteria invade the skin, potentially leading to a serious infection known as cellulitis.

I was moved to the pre-surgery ward where I shared a room with three elderly ladies. The first had a bowel issue, the second had emphysema, and the third had hypochondria. The hypochondriac was the most talkative of the three. The doctors were more than happy to discharge her, but she kept complaining of new ailments.

'Will you open this bottle of orange juice for me, darl?' she asked Geoff. 'My hands are riddled with arthritis.' Geoff obliged, before taking the opportunity to share the gospel with her.

I was wheeled to the operating theatre the following afternoon. In this vulnerable state, I can never decide where to direct my attention. Should I watch the orderly as he clumsily manoeuvres my bed down the hallway? Should I steal glances into the rooms as we pass them by? Or perhaps fidget with the hospital band around my wrist? It always feels so awkward.

The anaesthetist asked me the usual questions: *Do you know what operation you're about to have? Do you have any known allergies? Are you currently on any medications?*

Then he asked, 'You haven't eaten anything today, have you?'

'No. Well I had some apple juice a little while ago because the nurses told me to have some if my blood glucose levels went below 5.0.'

'Oh. They really shouldn't have told you that. You can't eat or drink anything at all. I'm sorry, but we won't be able to perform the operation for at least a few hours now.'

The next thing I knew I was bawling my eyes out. I was so over it. I wanted to go home.

I was rolled back to my room. The three elderly ladies saw me crying, but I didn't care. I lay on my side — the right side because it hurt too much to lie on the left — and shut my eyes. I was exhausted after a restless night, wanting nothing more than to fall asleep and wake up next to Geoff, snug in our bed in Collaroy Plateau.

Geoff was by my side when I woke up from my nap. His warm smile reassured me, putting me in much better spirits. I was soon transported under the fluorescent lights of the operating theatre again, and my thoughts spiralled to the worst possible case scenarios. But as the anaesthetist leaned over me, Psalm 56:3 came to mind: 'When I am afraid, I put my trust in you.'

Everything went black.

When I woke up from the surgery, I looked down at my leg and gasped when I saw a colossal bandage measuring twenty centimetres by ten centimetres. *How big is my scar going to be?!* A nurse noticed my distress and reassured me that the surgeons always use much larger bandages than they need to.

The surgeons came by the next morning to tell me that the surgery had gone according to plan. I was discharged from the hospital a couple of hours later with a strong painkiller called oxycodone. Geoff and I celebrated with brunch at one of our favourite cafés in Manly, Pure Wholefoods. The blueberry and coconut pancakes sure beat the hospital food I'd been eating over the past four days!

A nurse called me after I'd been home for a few days. 'The bacteria that caused your infection is called Methicillin-resistant *Staphylococcus Aureus*, or MRSA. The antibiotic you're currently on isn't strong enough to stop the infection. You need to go straight to your GP to get a prescription for a stronger antibiotic.'

Her voice faded as I tried to comprehend what she was telling me. I'm no doctor, but if I'd been prescribed the correct antibiotic in the first place, perhaps the surgery could have been avoided entirely.

Back home in the comfort of my own bed, I read a timely reminder in James 1:2-4: 'Consider it pure joy, my brothers and sisters, whenever you face trials of many kinds, because you know that the testing of your faith produces perseverance. Let perseverance finish its work so that you may be mature and complete, not lacking anything' (NIV).

When you run a marathon, you don't get a say in what the course will look like. There'll likely be sections you don't want to run, and you might find yourself complaining, *Why are the race directors making us climb this stupid hill when they could have easily chosen a path around it?* But as much as you may dislike the course, you can't take a shortcut or detour; otherwise you'll be disqualified.

Similarly, it's God who sets my course, and I must persevere through the challenges if I want to reach the finish line. Hebrews 12:1b-2 says, 'Let us run with endurance the race that is set before us, looking to Jesus, the founder and perfecter of our faith, who for the joy that was set before him endured the cross, despising the shame, and is seated at the right hand of the throne of God.'

On the marathon of life, encouragement can be found when we fix our eyes on Jesus. Jesus was whipped so severely that flesh was torn from His body. His face was beaten to the point that His beard was ripped from His face. A crown of thorns pierced His scalp. Nails were hammered through His wrists and feet.

And yet, remarkably, He was able to overcome this horrendous torture because of the joy set before Him. His eyes were firmly fixed on the finish line: Heaven — a place where we will live with God forever; a place where He will wipe away every tear from our eyes; a place where there will be no more death, or mourning, or crying, or pain (Revelation 21:3-4).

Having this injury sucked, but I decided to approach this setback as an opportunity for spiritual growth. Like Jesus, who blazed the trail before me, I looked beyond my temporary suffering to God's promise of eternal joy to come.

A community nurse visited me at home to change my dressing each morning. I averted my gaze, hesitant to look at my wound while she cleaned it out. I didn't want to be confronted with what Geoff described as a 'ghastly hole' in my leg.

One day he recorded a video of the nurse cleaning out the wound and filling it with medical gauze. He'd soon be doing this for me, and he didn't want to stuff it up. So as not to alarm me, he calmly told me, 'Don't worry. It doesn't look that bad.'

When I finally worked up the courage to look at it, I was horrified by what I saw. There was a *crater* in my leg. It was so deep that I couldn't see the bottom of it!

I'd ask the nurse the same question every morning: 'Can I run yet?' The response was always a resounding 'No'. I was bored out of my mind being stuck at home in bed. So, a few weeks after my surgery, I stopped asking her and went for a run. It was only a couple of kilometres, but it was exhilarating to be back on my feet again! I'd taken the gift of running for granted, not realising how blessed I was until it was taken away from me.

The next night, a fierce thunderstorm didn't stop Geoff and I from joining our local running club Pace Athletic on a hilly seven-kilometre run. We ran up and down the winding Snake Hill at Manly's North Head, with rain pelting down on us and thunder clapping in the not-too-distant distance. I was by far the slowest runner in the group, but I didn't care. I was running again!

I went for another run the next day, taking on the six-kilometre Long Reef loop. I surprised myself when I arrived home and realised I'd equalled my personal best time for the course — with a freaking hole in my leg! *I'm back, baby!*

CHAPTER 26

'Nothing significant is ever achieved from within one's comfort zone.'
—Greg Donovan

BIG RED RUN
DAY 4

5 July 2014

There's a post on the Big Red Run Facebook page today, calling for messages of support for the runners. I read the comments from friends and family on the big screen while soaking up the warmth of the campfire and eating my brekkie of instant porridge and banana.

I eagerly scan for a message from Geoff, and recognise his profile picture featuring a photo of us in front of the Sydney Harbour Bridge.

> *Go Cheekball. Climbing up the ladder slow and*
> *steady. Nice work. You're a-mazing!*

Despite feeling like I've been hit by a truck, his message helps me face the day with a smile on my face. It's encouraging to know he's following the updates online and cheering me on from almost two thousand kilometres away.

In the lead up to the race, Geoff tagged along on my training runs to support me. We had many unforgettable experiences, including one run where we were caught in a torrential storm, another where I was so dehydrated that we had to catch a bus back home from Chatswood, and one where I had a particularly debilitating hypo. Each of these 'bad' runs taught me lessons that have prepared me for the Big Red Run.

My legs feel like they're moving in slow motion as we set off at eight-thirty. Although I only have a 'short' distance of fifteen kilometres to cover, I predict it will be another tough day on the trails.

But I'm determined to keep moving, if only for the fact that a swarm of flies descends upon me every time I stand still. One of those daggy fly hats would be handy right about now! I pull my white and orange running buff up over my face to stop the flies from making a home in my nostrils or mouth.

I take a short break on top of one of the sand dunes, pausing to reflect on the journey God has placed me on. I'm in the middle of the Simpson Desert, running through uncharted landscapes that most people could never dream of, let alone experience firsthand.

It's impossible to explain this to someone who hasn't been there themselves, but the desert has a way of getting under your skin. Standing on that dune, looking out at the gibber plains on one side and the sparse, dry vegetation on the other, I feel like I could be the only person in the entire universe.

I laugh aloud when I read Geoff's note for the day:

During race day 4 — Steph is the best, chuck out the rest.

This is one of Geoff's trademark lines that he often writes in my birthday and anniversary cards. It makes me miss him even more if that's even possible.

A surge of joy runs through me when I see Dad set up at a marshalling point on his own about twelve kilometres into the course. I didn't know where he would be assigned today, so I wasn't sure when I would get to see him.

Dad slowly stands up from his fold-out camping chair as I approach. His clean-shaven face from day one is now peppered with brown and grey stubble, and he's sunburnt from being outdoors all morning. He takes off his sunglasses, and I notice big white circles around his eyes.

'You should probably put some sunscreen on, Dad!'

I chat with him for a while, before reluctantly saying goodbye. I don't get far before I realise that I can't see the next pink flag. I was recently diagnosed with short-sighted vision, but I haven't yet bought a pair of prescription glasses. *Where the dickens is it?* I pace back and forth trying to find it, asking God to guide me the right way. Soon enough, I spot the next flag and move towards it.

I finish the day's fifteen kilometres in a time of 2:18:38. I run into camp dirty, dusty, starving, and shattered. I take off my shoes to shake out the sand, and carefully peel off the adhesive tape I've wrapped around my toes to prevent blisters. I notice that two small blisters have formed, one on my right pinkie toe and the other on my left heel. They're nowhere near as bad as some of the ones I've seen on the feet of other runners!

On the eve of the Big Red Run, the event safety manager Lucas Trihey gave us a lengthy tutorial on what to do to both prevent and treat blisters. If anyone knows anything about blisters, it's Lucas. In 2006, he was the first person to walk unassisted across the Simpson Desert, pulling a purpose-built cart behind him with all his food, water, and supplies. He walked an incredible four hundred kilometres over seventeen days!

So, I take Lucas' advice and carefully pop my blisters with a clean needle, drain all the fluid out, and cover them with band-aids. It's gross, but sometimes you've gotta do what you've gotta do.

🏃 🏃 🏃

Chilling in the tent with Dad each afternoon has become the highlight of my time in Birdsville. We zip up the screen to keep the flies at bay and spread out on our self-inflating mattresses, exhausted from the day's effort. We debrief on what we've each been up to, bonding over our fatigue and how annoying the flies are.

I feel blessed to have Dad here to cook me warm, hearty meals on our portable stove each night. Most of the runners don't have that luxury, having travelled to Birdsville on their own via plane or bus, with a fourteen-kilogram baggage restriction. Because we travelled up in Dad's Hilux, we have access to our own portable fridge to store fresh fruit and bread, and to keep milk and Pepsi Max cool.

While I feast on Dad's delicious meals, the other runners are eating unappetising freeze-dried meals. In fairness, I need the fridge to store my insulin. Temperatures in the Simpson Desert can drop below zero degrees Celsius, and insulin loses its effectiveness when it freezes.

Dad and I also have a tent to ourselves, whereas the other runners have to share a tent with up to three others. I'm especially grateful when I hear stories around the campfire of a certain runner who snores so loudly that he's been mistaken for a dying cow.

By this stage, I am well and truly longing to put on clean clothes. The unpleasant stench of mine and Dad's feet in the socks we've worn for four days straight lingers in the air of our tent (why we didn't pack more pairs, I'll never know). There are obviously no showers in the middle of the desert, so the only thing we have to keep ourselves from stinking the place out is deodorant and wet wipes. Of course, these can only go so far.

I desperately need to wash my hair too. It's so greasy from all the sweat I've expelled over the last few days. I'm too embarrassed to be seen without either my purple beanie or white Big Red Run hat on. Many of the other runners use their buffs to do the same. But I try to stay positive, knowing that I'm only two sleeps away from being back in civilisation.

Mum posted a message on my Facebook page yesterday, but I haven't had reception to read it until this afternoon:

> *You've done over seventy kilometres and you still have energy to take selfies! What a champion daughter I have! Amazing the stamina you have. Must've got it from your mother. So proud of you for doing this Steph. Tell Dad I'm surviving quite well on Lean Cuisine dinners. Not as good as his meals but they are keeping me alive so I can do all your washing when you get back. Team effort.*

CHAPTER 27

'It's very hard in the beginning to understand that the whole idea is not to beat the other runners. Eventually you learn that the competition is against the little voice inside you that wants you to quit.'
—George Sheehan

9 April – 21 May 2017

I ran the half marathon at the Australian Running Festival just two and a half months after the surgery on my thigh. I searched the crowd for the sub two-hour pacers at the start line. There's something special about being part of a group of runners who share the same goal, motivating one another to achieve it together.

I quickly spotted blue flags fluttering in the sky with the words, *Two hours.*

'Want to run with us?' asked a pacer with a friendly grin.

'Yes, please!'

I'd been on track to run my first sub two-hour half marathon prior to the surgery, but I doubted whether I could still do it because I'd been unable to keep up with my training program. I would have been happy to simply break my previous personal best of 2:06:52.

Quite soon into the race, I found myself edging ahead of the pacers on the downhill from Parliament House. I knew it was a risk to go out too hard, but I thought they were running *way* too slow for how good I was feeling that morning. The risk paid off; I managed to stay ahead of them the entire way, finishing the 21.1 kilometres in a time of 1:58:53, and beating my previous personal best by eight minutes.

Six weeks later, I took another three minutes off my personal best when I ran the Sydney Morning Herald Half Marathon in 1:55:40. I was at my peak and thought, *What better time to take on my next marathon?*

The Irish middle distance runner Noel Carroll said, 'If people were possessed by reason, running marathons would not work. But we are not creatures of reason. We are creatures of passion.' My passion for running was stronger than ever, and I was ready to take on the highs and lows of marathon training once again.

29 June 2017

I signed up for the Gold Coast Marathon, famous for its super flat and fast course alongside the city's renowned surf beaches. The race attracts thousands of runners from around the globe, thanks to its ideal winter running conditions, with nearly a quarter of participants achieving personal bests each year.

My goal was to run a sub four-hour marathon. I knew it would be difficult (only twenty-one per cent of female marathon runners finish in less than four hours), but I also knew it was possible if I put in the work. I increased the time on my feet, logging up to sixty kilometres per week. I was blessed to have Geoff to keep me company — not to mention sane — on the longer runs.

After a six-hour delay, Geoff and I boarded our first ever flight together to the Gold Coast. Geoff had registered for the 5.7-kilometre fun run, and Rob had flown all the way from New Zealand to take on his second half marathon.

We arranged to meet Rob at the tourist hot spot of Cavill Avenue, lined with an array of souvenir shops, nightclubs, tattoo parlours, and restaurants. The eye-catching *Surfers Paradise* sign stood at the end of the street as a perfect backdrop to the famous golden sand and turquoise waters of Surfers Paradise.

A street performer balancing on stilts towered over a captivated audience. Rob easily stood out from the crowd thanks to his distinctive gnome-like appearance, and we were soon catching up and carb loading together.

2 July 2017

When race morning arrived, fellow coffee addict Rob and I made a beeline for a café near the start line for our mandatory caffeine fix. Coffee has this magical ability to both make you feel invincible and calm your nerves. It never feels right when I arrive at a race without having had coffee first, in the same way that it wouldn't feel right if I turned up without a sports bra on.

I foolishly began the race with a pace there was no feasible way I'd be able to sustain for 42.195 kilometres. I caught sight of my Big Red Run friends Phill and Ricky ahead and picked up the pace even more to catch up to them. Chatting with them made the time speed past and I was feeling great. I technically ran my fastest ever half marathon, completing the first 21.1 kilometres in an incredible 1:52:12. Incredible for me, anyway.

One spectator after another yelled out, 'Go Steph!' I was confused about how they all knew my name until I remembered that it was printed on the front of my race bib. I loved seeing the joy on the faces of kids lining the streets, reaching out an expectant hand for a high-five. Slapping my sweaty hand against theirs gave me that extra burst of energy I needed to keep pushing ahead.

However, it wasn't long before I hit 'the wall' — that dreaded point around thirty-two kilometres into a marathon when your legs feel like lead, your energy depletes to near non-existence, and even your brain starts to shut down. Self-doubt crept into my thoughts, and reaching the finish line seemed insurmountable.

'You're almost there, Steph!' shout spectators with takeaway coffee cups and handmade signs.

Ten kilometres is not *almost there!* I think, shuffling along in self-pity.

But what the brain thinks is the limit often isn't the truth for the body, and I kept going, knocking over the wall with all the strength I had left in me.

Geoff was waiting with his dad John a couple of hundred metres from the finish line in Southport. Their encouragement spurred me on, and I managed a sprint finish to the end. When I say 'sprint', I mean I picked up the pace slightly, but I was still slower than a turtle wading through peanut butter.

With dance music blaring over the sound of the crowd's cheers, I completed the race in an official time of 4:08:44. I hadn't achieved my target time of sub four hours, but I was ecstatic that I'd smashed my personal best marathon time by over thirty minutes!

CHAPTER 28

'In the dust of defeat as well as the laurels of victory, there is glory to be found if one has done his best.'
—Eric Liddell

13 August 2017

When I lined up at the start line of the 2017 City2Surf, I was a completely transformed person from the one I was at my first City2Surf in 2009. Not only was I fitter and at least eight kilograms lighter, but I was also a much happier and more confident person.

As I waited at the start line, surrounded by 80,000 eager faces, the atmosphere was electric. I glanced down at my insulin pump to see that my blood glucose level was 10.1. A little high, but nothing unexpected given the adrenaline surging through my body.

The gun sounded and we were off, running downhill on William Street before heading up through the tunnel at Kings Cross. Knowing what lay ahead, I concentrated on pacing myself so I wouldn't burn out too quickly.

It was my first time wearing a costume at a race, and I felt encouraged as the spectators cheered, 'Go Super Girl!' I wasn't the only runner dressed up in a costume. I couldn't help but giggle when I saw Forrest Gump, dressed in a red cap, yellow shirt, and red shorts, with a beard that cascaded down his chin.

I felt like I was flying as I looked out over the picturesque Rose Bay. My hill training had paid off; I powered up the notorious Heartbreak Hill at the halfway mark. Approaching the turn at Vaucluse, I caught my first glimpse of the ocean. *Woohoo! Finally on the homestretch!*

'It's all downhill from here!' called out an elderly man at one of the water stations. My cape billowed behind me as I dodged and weaved between my fellow runners, heading downhill towards Bondi. I made sure not to run too closely behind anyone in case they stopped suddenly to take a selfie or catch their breath.

I smiled as I crossed the finish line at Bondi Beach in a time of 1:16:55 — my fastest ever City2Surf! I beat my personal best time by over seven minutes. Even better, I finished with a perfect blood glucose reading of 6.8.

Mum, Geoff and I chilled out in the Too Many Pricks tent after the race, eating sausage sandwiches on the sandy shores of Bondi Beach. Too Many Pricks is an awesome not-for-profit organisation with the slogan, 'For everyone living with type 1 diabetes, life is full of too many pricks.'

Their cheeky name refers to finger pricks, and their mission is to raise both funds and awareness for type 1 diabetes by bringing the community together to participate in challenging activities. It was fantastic to kick back and unwind after such a big effort, while connecting with other like-minded individuals living with type 1 diabetes.

17 September 2017

I found myself in the heart of Sydney, admiring the iconic Sydney Harbour Bridge as it elegantly arched over the sparkling waterfront. There was a chill in the air, giving me goose bumps from head to toe. I sat in the Guylian

Café, right near the finish line of the Sydney Running Festival at the Opera House in Circular Quay, warming my hands with my cappuccino.

Thousands of people of all shapes, sizes, and backgrounds were running past me, each in a different season of life and with their own goals, expectations, and motivations for being there. They each had their own unique running form. Some sprinted to the finish like the Flash as though their lives depended on getting a personal best, their faces squinched up like they were in unbearable pain; others hobbled along with beaming smiles.

Some were dressed up as Disney princesses with glittery tiaras and tutus, or superheroes with masks and capes; others wore expensively branded race gear from head to toe. Some were running their first ever race, taking the very first steps on their fitness journey; others were running for competition — either against themselves or against others.

Some were running to raise money for a charity close to their heart; others were running because they were keen to impress their crush. When the gun went off, they all followed the same course to the finish, but each of them had taken a different path to the start line.

As for me, I was content to enjoy the atmosphere while waiting for Geoff to finish his five-kilometre race. I finished my coffee and walked over to the steps of the Opera House. I overheard a group of runners talking about the highlights and lowlights of the run with their family and friends. Some were making excuses for their 'poor' performances, while others shared a sense of accomplishment at achieving a new personal best time.

Speed is relative. For some, an eight-minute kilometre is 'slow', but for others, it could well represent years and years of hard work. I used to compare myself with faster runners until I realised that, at the end of the day, no one actually cares what my pace is except me! So now I make a conscious effort not to worry about what others are thinking, and to instead strive for *my* best.

I saw a young boy wearing a striped shirt and khaki pants racing away from his mum. 'Come here, sweetie,' she called, desperate not to lose her son in the crowd. I questioned whether I was ready to tackle the responsibilities of motherhood, and realised I already had so much to be thankful for — a husband who loves me and would do anything for me; a family who will always be there for me; friends who make me laugh and whom I can share life with.

Among the cheers of the spectators, I heard a British accent say, 'Do you mind taking a photo of me?'

I turn around to see a gorgeous twenty-something lady with blonde hair, wearing tight-fitting Lorna Jane active wear. She was holding her iPhone out in front of her and gesturing towards the Opera House.

'Of course!'

She posed with the race medal between her lips as I snapped photos of her, the sunshine shimmering off the sails of the Opera House in the background. As I handed her phone back, I glimpsed Geoff in the corner of my eye.

I ran over and embraced him, doing my best to ignore the sweat soaking his red T-shirt.

'I'm so proud of you, Cheekball!'

I had no idea what time he finished in; it didn't matter. He got out there and did his best, and that's what counts.

CHAPTER 29

*'Two things are infinite: the universe and human
stupidity; and I'm not sure about the universe.'*
—Albert Einstein

26 December 2017 – 2 January 2018

In October 2017, I registered for the ultimate dream destination race: the
Walt Disney World Marathon in Orlando, Florida. Having grown up with
a fondness for all things Disney, watching VHS tapes of *Beauty and the
Beast* and *Snow White and the Seven Dwarfs* on repeat, I'd wanted to do this
race since I first started running.

When a link popped up in my Facebook news feed, I couldn't resist
clicking on it. I saw that tickets were almost sold out (or so the website
claimed). I'm a spontaneous person, as evidenced by my decision to sign
up that same day.

'Can I *please* do the Walt Disney World Marathon?' I begged Geoff. 'I
promise I'll never ask for anything else ever again.'

I managed to convince him... on the condition that I sell my beloved
Mitsubishi Mirage to help fund the trip. A couple of days later, we booked
flights for a five and a half week, 8,000-kilometre — or should I say 5,000-
mile? — road trip across the United States of America. We arrived at Sydney

International Airport on Boxing Day, packed and ready for the adventure of a lifetime.

Our trip kicked off with a series of unfortunate events. First, I misplaced our Travelex Mastercard, loaded with all our holiday funds, during our stopover at Auckland International Airport. I must have put it down when I was buying something at one of the duty-free stores. I didn't realise I'd left it until we were on the flight to Los Angeles.

We called Auckland Airport's Lost and Found as soon as we landed, and they informed us that someone had generously handed the card in. Although it was incredibly inconvenient, we were able to access money by ordering 'emergency cash' to be sent to certain Western Union locations.

We arrived in New York City at six in the morning after over twenty hours of flying and a lengthy stopover in Los Angeles. After half an hour of watching one suitcase after another move past us on the conveyor belt, we were still waiting for our baggage to appear. I walked over to the lady at the information desk to ask about it.

'Do you have the baggage claim number they gave you when you checked in?' she asked.

'Um, I didn't get one,' I said.

'If you don't have a number, there's nothing I can do to track down your bags.'

She remained nonchalant; I, on the other hand, was panicking. *What will we do if our bags are missing?* Stupidly, we didn't pack any warm clothes in our carry-on baggage, so we were stuck in T-shirts and shorts in freezing New York! I walked back to Geoff in hysterics.

'Our bags are missing!' I was jet lagged and keen to get to our airbnb to catch up on sleep.

I sighed with relief when the airport staff located our bags an hour or so later, offering no explanation for why they weren't on the conveyor belt with the others.

A blast of icy air struck my cheeks as we walked through the airport doors onto a bustling street, where a grumpy taxi driver soon ripped us off.

Things went from bad to worse. Before we left for our trip, Geoff saw an ad on Craigslist for a brown 2002 Dodge Caravan. In true Cheekball style, we wanted a car we could sleep in, so we decided it would be perfect for us. How did I not register that something was dodgy when I read the ad with its lack of grammar and punctuation?!

car runs and drives great everything works no mechanical issues no warning lights no leaks tires brakes battery oil recently done Great on gas clean title must-see and drive $1500.

Geoff called the number and spoke to a man named Ray Green. Ray assured Geoff that he owned a reputable used car sales business, and that the car was in top condition. He said that it came with temporary registration for a month, but he was happy to extend it for an additional month for us.

When we arrived in New York, Geoff organised to meet Ray's nephew, John, to pick up the car in Brooklyn. However, the address John gave us wasn't his home. We discovered this when we knocked on the door, and the man who lived there said, 'No, there's no John here. Are you sure you have the right address?'

It turned out John was waiting in a car parked close by. He gave Geoff the title for the car, claiming that was all we'd need to transfer the car ownership over to us. So we handed John $1,500 in cash, waved goodbye, and drove towards our airbnb in Manhattan. We didn't get far before we noticed that smoke was billowing from the engine, and there was no heat coming from the air conditioning vents!

We had the car inspected by a mechanic named Jose the following day. He told us the car had major mechanical issues, and that we'd need to replace the radiator if we wanted to drive it safely. Geoff called Ray and spoke to him about the issues with the car, and Ray agreed to pay for the repairs.

While we waited for the car to be fixed, we visited New York City's popular tourist attractions. We rode a ferry across to the Statue of Liberty, took the elevator to the one hundred and second floor of the Empire State Building, appreciated artworks by Monet and van Gogh at the Metropolitan Museum of Modern Art, watched a production called *C.S. Lewis On Stage: The Most Reluctant Convert* in Times Square, and marvelled at the enormous Christmas tree display at the Rockefeller Centre.

The east coast's record low temperatures meant we wore almost every layer of clothing we'd packed. The temperature dropped to minus thirteen degrees Celsius on New Year's Eve! Our staple comfort food became hot soup, and we sampled the options at Soup Kitchen International, a little takeaway shop made famous by the classic *Seinfeld* episode, 'The Soup Nazi'.

When we returned to pick up the car a few days later, Jose said, 'You should take the car back to Ray. He shouldn't have sold it to you in this condition.'

By this stage, Ray had stopped replying to Geoff's phone calls and text messages. For all we knew, his nephew 'John' could have been Ray himself!

We drove to an address in Queens that was listed on the original Craigslist ad, only to discover it was a fake address and not the location of a used car sales business after all. There were, however, other vehicles for sale parked in the vicinity, with similar signage to that on the one we'd purchased. We also realised that the picture of the car in the ad wasn't the one we bought, but a remarkably similar one!

Until this day, Geoff says it was so unlike him to go through with the purchase, and that it's 'possibly the stupidest thing' he's ever done.

CHAPTER 30

'All our dreams can come true, if we have the courage to pursue them.'
—Walt Disney

3 – 6 January 2018

We left New York two days later than we'd originally planned due to the issues with the car. This left us only four days to drive 1,700 kilometres to Orlando to arrive in time for the Walt Disney World Marathon. I was disappointed that we'd have to miss out on so many of the places we had on our original itinerary.

We folded down the seats in the back of the Dodge Caravan, bought a couple of pieces of timber from a hardware store, and placed a cheap mattress from Walmart on top. One of the greatest challenges was working out how to keep my insulin from freezing. I'd sleep with the vials in my pockets, or wrap them up in beanies and scarves overnight.

In Philadelphia, we were lame and jogged up the 'Rocky Steps'. The actor Sylvester Stallone, playing Rocky Balboa, famously ran up the stairs of the Philadelphia Museum of Art in the first *Rocky* film, and it's become a popular tourist attraction ever since.

Dozens of people from different nations were there, puffing as they jogged up and down the stairs, their faces flushed with effort as they punched their fists in the air upon reaching the top.

7 January 2018

The morning of the marathon finally arrived. I stood shivering at the start line at five thirty, bouncing from one foot to the other to stop myself from freezing to death in the winter chill. I was pumped when an explosion of fireworks lit up the pre-dawn sky above. Americans sure know how to go all-out!

The 42.195-kilometre course snaked through the entire Walt Disney World Resort, passing through each of the four theme parks: Epcot, Magic Kingdom, Animal Kingdom, and Hollywood Studios. I'd let my training slide since landing in the United States, and it showed on race day. I think the only run we did was a one-kilometre jog through Central Park in New York City, and the only reason we ran was because we were running late to a comedy show in Times Square.

Needless to say, I was in a universe of pain very early into the race. It was tricky to get my head around the fact that the distance markers were in miles rather than kilometres. When you're fatigued and not the best at maths as it is, it doesn't come easily to convert between the two measurements.

The Walt Disney World Marathon was unlike any race I've ever participated in. I didn't care how fast — or slow — I was going; I was only focused on enjoying the journey. Running through Cinderella's Castle was like being in a fairytale. Soaking in the cheers from the stadium bleachers at the ESPN Wide World of Sports was a dream come true. And I couldn't keep the smile off my face when I came across people dressed up as different Disney characters every couple of kilometres.

The time flew by, and I didn't pay much attention to the numbers on my Garmin. I finished in a time of 5:06:56, which stands as my slowest marathon to date. Even still, I placed in the top twenty per cent of female finishers, and top thirty per cent of all finishers, which just goes to show that the race is much more about having fun and making memories than it is about competition.

My finisher's medal was nothing short of magical. In typical American fashion, it was at least double the size of every other medal I've ever received, with shiny gold glitter all over it. There was a spinning Mickey Mouse in the centre, with a quote by Walt Disney: *If you can dream it, you can do it.* So far it's the only medal I've received from an overseas race, but I certainly hope it's not the last!

9 – 27 January 2018

Over the following two weeks, we drove the length of the United States from Florida to California. We tasted local beer in Pensacola, Florida, and gumbo in New Orleans, Louisiana. We spray painted Cadillacs buried nose-first in the dirt in Amarillo, Texas, on the famous Route 66. We stood on the rim of a 1.2-kilometre-wide, 170-metre-deep meteorite crater in Flagstaff, Arizona. We were captivated by the most breathtaking sunset over the majestic Grand Canyon in the north-west corner of Arizona. We had fun hitting the Vegas Strip and seeing the flashing neon signs in Las Vegas, Nevada.

After an action-packed couple of weeks, we spent a few days with my friend Janani in San Francisco, California. Janani and I were best friends in primary school. We lost touch when she moved to Bangalore, India, at the end of 1999. She had posted a letter to me, however I'd moved to a new house in the next suburb during the school holidays, so it never reached me.

It wasn't until I joined Facebook in 2008 that I was able to reconnect with Janani. We stayed in contact through regular emails, discussing topics ranging from Philosophy and Science to religion and health.

In August 2009, before starting my exchange program in England, Melissa and I travelled around the United Kingdom together. Janani just so happened to be studying in Edinburgh, Scotland, at that time, so we seized the opportunity to visit her. I saw her again when I travelled to Bengaluru, as she happened to be there on a short holiday to visit her family at the same time!

I couldn't go all the way to the United States and not visit her in San Francisco. Together, we wandered the Muir Woods National Monument, craning our necks to take in the colossal thousand-year-old redwood trees that towered 250 feet above us (that's roughly equivalent to stacking a six-foot-tall person head to toe forty-five times!).

28 – 31 January 2018

The final destination of our epic road trip was Los Angeles. We stayed with our friend Marnie, who kindly showed us around the sprawling city with its famous 90210 postcode. She drove us up to the Griffith Observatory overlooking the white Hollywood Sign which I'd seen in many films and television shows since I was a little girl.

Alas, Geoff sprained his ankle on our second day in Los Angeles. I'm sure he wishes there was an interesting story behind the injury, but the truth is he tripped and fell down a single stair in Marnie's garage. He spent the rest of the holiday shuffling around with a moonboot and crutches, and we were forced to skip our planned activities.

We didn't miss our tour of the Living Waters headquarters though. Living Waters is a ministry that inspires and equips Christians to fulfil the Great Commission to go and tell the world about Jesus (Matthew 28:19-20). The Founder and CEO, Ray Comfort, is a Kiwi-born minister, best-selling author, and film producer, who has dedicated his life to sharing the good news of Jesus with everyone he meets.

We were blessed to have the opportunity to meet Ray while we were on the tour. He noticed our Aussie accents immediately; the fact that I greeted him with 'G'day!' must have given it away. As busy as his schedule was, Ray spent over an hour with us. He gave us a behind-the-scenes look at a brand-new film that hadn't been released yet. He even showed us his office, where he had us in hysterics with jokes that covered the walls from floor to ceiling.

'This is a picture of my three kids,' Ray said, pointing at a photo of three people with his own moustached face superimposed onto each of them. 'I've got three. One of each. My daughter looks amazingly like me as you can see.'

There was also a photo of Ray hugging an orangutan. 'Here's a photo of me with my nephew, Esau. Hairy little fellow.' He was referring to Esau from the Bible, who is described in Genesis 25:25 as 'red, all his body like a hairy cloak'.

'Now, everyone's got one of these,' he said, opening a closet to reveal a life-size human skeleton.

'And here we have a map of Australia and New Zealand as they are in truth.' It was a drawing of New Zealand, with the islands labelled *North Island* and *South Island*, alongside a much smaller image of Australia labelled *West Island*.

🏃 🏃 🏃

Before we left to fly home to Australia, we asked Ray Comfort if his ministry had any need for our Dodge Caravan. It ended up being a good thing that he politely turned down our offer. Instead, we left the car with Marnie to sell on our behalf. Our poor friend was out driving it one day when she was pulled over and arrested by police officers with guns drawn! Not surprisingly, Ray Green had lied to us about the car being registered, and it was in fact a stolen vehicle!

CHAPTER 31

*'For everything there is a season, and a time
for every matter under heaven.'*
—Ecclesiastes 3:1

February 2016 – February 2018

In the two years following my miscarriages, I experienced many phantom pregnancy symptoms. I wanted a baby so desperately that I'd convince myself that I was pregnant every time I felt bloated or more tired than usual. Of course, these can also be symptoms of an impending period. I hate to think how much money I spent on pregnancy tests during this time!

Patience is something I struggle with big time. I often catch myself running ahead of God, propelled by my desire for an immediate result. I wondered why it was taking so long to fall pregnant again. I wanted a baby, and I wanted a baby *now*! It seemed so effortless before. I only needed to *look* at Geoff and I'd get pregnant.

Instead of counting my chickens and merely assuming that my fertility was okay, I counted my *eggs*. Women are born with their lifetime supply of eggs, and these gradually decrease in both quality and quantity as they age. So I took an Ovarian Reserve Test (sometimes called the 'Egg Timer Test'), which measures the level of anti-mullerian hormones in your blood.

In other words, it can indicate how many eggs you have remaining in your ovaries, and therefore how many more fertile years you have.

'Your levels are slightly below the average for someone your age,' said my GP. 'You still have time to get pregnant, so don't worry. But I wouldn't put it off if I were you.'

Trust me, I'm not trying to put it off, I thought to myself. My biological clock had been ticking for over a decade. Even though I was almost thirty and still being asked for ID when I bought alcohol, I didn't exactly *feel* young anymore.

My GP gave me referrals for a blood test to check important pregnancy hormones like progesterone, and an internal pelvic ultrasound to make sure my ovaries, uterus and fallopian tubes were working as they should. But everything came back normal.

'Do you wish you hadn't married me?' I asked Geoff one night.

'Why do you ask that?'

'Because I might not be able to give you children.'

I knew how much Geoff had always wanted to have a daughter. I couldn't help but wonder, *What if I can't give him what he wants? Will he resent me for the rest of his life?*

Geoff gently unfolded the pages of his weathered Bible, its spine fraying from years of devoted study. He read Job 1:21: '"Naked I came from my mother's womb, and naked shall I return. The LORD gave, and the LORD has taken away; blessed be the name of the LORD." Only God can give us children, Cheekball. Just trust Him.'

He was right, of course. Everything that was happening to me was happening only by the will of God. He allows bad things to happen, but I have His promise in Romans 8:28 that 'in all things God works for the good of those who love him, who have been called according to his purpose.'

I prayed that God would heal me of any potential fertility issues, reminding myself that sometimes He answers me with a 'Yes', sometimes it's a 'No', and sometimes it's 'Wait'. I was thankful for the unmistakable nearness of God in this wilderness of uncertainty.

5 March 2018

On the fifth of March, I headed out for my first run since the Walt Disney World Marathon two months earlier. But as soon as I started, a sharp pain shot through my right knee. I limped along for a couple of kilometres, but was forced to slow to a walk, confused and frustrated by the intensity of the pain.

I had an MRI scan the following day which diagnosed a 'chronic anterior cruciate ligament tear and full-thickness loss of articular cartilage'. In more understandable terms, thanks to Doctor Google, I had a tear in one of the knee ligaments that joined my thigh and shin bones. This had caused my knee to become unstable and my bones to rub against each other, causing damage to the tissue that cushioned my knee joint.

In slightly more understandable terms, my knee was stuffed.

An orthopaedic specialist told me, 'It's not a good idea to keep running long distances with your knee the way it is. You'll need surgery to reconstruct the anterior cruciate ligament.'

I still had so many running goals I wanted to achieve in the future. *What choice do I have?*

Besides, what's another scar or three to add to my growing list? I used to be so self-conscious of my scars, but now I like to think that each of them tells a story. They might be unsightly, but they're proof that I've lived an interesting life.

I've lost count of how many I have now. There's the one on my right shin from when I stacked it on slippery steel stairs at Manly Dam. The wound became infected and oozed so much yellow pus that I convinced myself I'd get gangrene and need to get my leg amputated.

There's the faint, white scar from that rusty fence on day three of the Big Red Run. There's the couple on my left knee from falling over right at the end of a seven-kilometre run at Centennial Park, just two metres from where I'd parked my car! There's the pair of centimetre-long scars on my right knee from my first arthroscopic knee surgery. And let's not forget the one midway up my left thigh from when the abscess was cut out.

I hear you say, 'Well, it serves you right! Running is bad for your knees.' You might be surprised to learn that this common belief is nothing more than an old wives' tale. In fact, studies have shown that runners have healthier bones and joints than those who don't run!

Far from causing wear and tear on our knees, running for thirty minutes a day lowers inflammation in knee joints, which may help to *prevent* injuries and arthritis. Research suggests that you're more likely to develop arthritis if you're carrying extra weight and have a sedentary lifestyle.

Strangely enough, I don't know what caused the actual tear to my anterior cruciate ligament. After my knee arthroscopy in 2006, I was told that it had been stretched, but there was no urgent need to replace it then.

I suspect the actual tear happened when I landed awkwardly on a friend's trampoline in late 2015. I couldn't walk properly for weeks. I was pregnant at the time, and I learned that pregnancy makes women more susceptible to injuries due to the production of progesterone and relaxin. These hormones prepare the body for childbirth by relaxing muscles and loosening ligaments and joints, particularly in the pelvis and, in my case, the knee.

CHAPTER 32

'The heart of man plans his way, but the LORD establishes his steps.'
—Proverbs 16:9

4 – 5 April 2018

On the morning of my surgery, an admission nurse put a white hospital band on my wrist.

'You're not diabetic, are you?' she asked.

'I am actually,' I replied.

The nurse sighed, cut off the wristband with scissors, and replaced it with a red one, the colour used for patients with diabetes. She stamped every page of my files with the word *DIABETIC* in red ink. I've never seen someone stamp as aggressively as she did! There was a loud *bang* and the whole desk would shake every time the stamp hit the page. *It's not my fault I have diabetes, lady!*

After the surgery, when the anaesthetic had worn off, I checked my phone to see a text message from Melissa:

It's so weird. I have excruciating pain in my knee right now!

She said she'd never had pain like that before. It was in her left knee, but interestingly, Melissa is left-handed while I'm right-handed. If that's not proof of the special connection between identical twins, I don't know what is.

The recovery for this surgery was far more challenging than my thigh surgery the previous year — at least I could go to the toilet on my own then! This time, I had to press a buzzer every time I needed to go. Nothing gives you a crash course in humility quite like having a nurse remove a bedpan full of your excrement from beneath you.

A transparent tube protruded from my leg, and I could see dark red blood flowing through it. 'Okay, I'm going to pull this out now,' said a nurse. I couldn't bring myself to watch as she yanked the tube free. It was the strangest feeling!

I had the worst sleep of my entire life that night. A nurse woke me up every couple of hours to measure my blood pressure and temperature, and to check what my blood glucose levels were. Even when I was alone in the room, the agony in my knee and relentless beeping of machines kept me awake.

The following morning, Mum drove all the way from Wattle Grove in peak hour traffic to be there when I was discharged. Geoff knew she was coming and had kept it a secret from me. I was not at all expecting to see her, but it didn't surprise me because I knew she'd want to be there for me, as she always is.

The surgeon had given me a DVD of the operation to watch back later, like a souvenir of my visit to the hospital. I had no intention of watching it any time soon, but Mum and Geoff wanted to put it on as soon as we got home. I viewed it with my hands over my face, taking quick glimpses between my fingers. It was like a scene straight out of a gory horror film — except I was the one being hacked up and drilled into.

7 – 24 April 2018

Geoff and I weren't actively trying to fall pregnant in March, and I was losing hope that it would happen again. Besides, we didn't think it would be a good idea for me to go under general anaesthetic while I was pregnant, or to have to worry about how my blood glucose levels would affect a baby, knowing that it would be difficult to keep them stable while my body was under so much stress.

A few days after the surgery, I had a sense that I might be pregnant. I asked Geoff to buy me a pregnancy test on our way home from a physiotherapy appointment. He couldn't deny that my boobs looked bigger, so this time he didn't complain that the test was a waste of money.

I took the test as soon as we arrived home. I sat next to Geoff on the couch, holding the test in my hand. We looked down at it and, sure enough, two pink lines appeared almost instantly. I couldn't believe it — I was pregnant!

'It's funny that the physio today said it'll be nine months until you can run again. Might as well have a baby in the meantime,' Geoff said.

'Might as well!' I laughed.

I was worried because I'd consumed quite a bit of alcohol over the previous few weeks, having no reason to think I could be pregnant. Mum and I had shared a bottle of Cabernet Sauvignon that my family had gifted me as a 'Get Well Soon' present on the day after my surgery.

We nicknamed the baby 'Chickpea'. At our dating scan, the sonographer asked me to hold my breath so she could pick up the baby's pulse. She didn't need to ask; I was already holding it. I waited for her to say, 'There's no heartbeat.' But she didn't — there was a tiny heartbeat!

3 – 17 May 2018

I had my first appointment with Dr Smith when I was eight weeks pregnant. I sat in the waiting room with Geoff, absentmindedly chewing on my fingernails.

'I'm so scared,' I told him, my clammy hand in his. I feared that something had happened to the baby since our last scan. I figured I should have experienced at least *some* morning sickness by now.

'Congratulations!' Dr Smith beamed, his tall frame bending down to envelope me in a warm hug. I smiled back, but it did little to disguise my anxiety.

'You're making *me* nervous!' Dr Smith said. 'Come through and we'll take a look at your baby.'

I blinked away tears as Dr Smith prepped the ultrasound equipment. But when the probe was on my abdomen and I looked up at the screen, our baby came into view. My jaw dropped open as I stared at the head, spine, arms, and legs, all perfectly formed. The only word I could think to say was, 'Wow!'

'There's a very healthy heartbeat, guys — 164 beats per minute. You don't have anything to worry about.'

I hadn't made it this far into a pregnancy before. Day by day, we surpassed the timelines of our previous pregnancies. Eight weeks. Nine weeks. Ten weeks. I feared another failed pregnancy, so I made no mention to Geoff about my ideas for the baby's nursery, and I didn't dare buy any baby clothes.

On the seventeenth of May, when I was eleven weeks pregnant, I started bleeding. It took a while for it to sink in — the possibility that I was miscarrying again. When it did, I buried my face in Geoff's chest and broke down.

CHAPTER 33

*'Do not worry about tomorrow, for tomorrow will worry
about itself. Each day has enough trouble of its own.'*
—Matthew 6:34 (NIV)

18 – 21 May 2018

'Stephanie Walters?' A blonde sonographer waited for me, holding a file containing reports about my previous pregnancies and the babies I'd lost.

'Congratulations on your pregnancy!' she smiled.

'Um, thanks. Actually, I had some bleeding yesterday.'

She did her best to reassure me that bleeding during pregnancy can be normal. But this 'normal' had always been a precursor to grief in the past, so I didn't get my hopes up as she moved the cold probe over my abdomen.

Finally, after an eternity, I heard it — a strong heartbeat of 153 beats per minute. Instead of the tears of sadness I'd prepared myself for, I cried tears of happiness. I saw our baby wiggling around, his or her tiny hand reaching up and waving as if sharing our joy.

A few days later, I received a phone call from Dad. Once again, I assumed he would only have bad news to share.

'I'm sorry, Steph. Papou passed away.'

Papou had been in hospital for the past couple of weeks due to an infection, followed by a stroke. The doctors were in disbelief that he lived as long as he did once his organs began to shut down. It didn't surprise my family though; Papou had always been a fighter.

Tears instantly filled my eyes when I got off the phone with Dad. Papou had recently told Mum that he was 'ready to go be with Yiayia', but knowing this didn't make things easier. Memories of Papou dancing and singing to traditional Greek music in my grandparents' Hurlstone Park home came flooding back to me.

What a roller coaster of emotions I was on! From fear and worry to joy and relief over our little Chickpea, followed by deep sorrow for the loss of a grandfather I loved so dearly. I worried that crying too violently would affect the baby, but I didn't know how to stop.

🏃 🏃 🏃

12 – 21 June 2018

I had bleeding off and on in the weeks following Papou's death. Negative thoughts consumed me: *Will* this *baby survive? Will we finally get our miracle?* Surely we hadn't come this close to the 'safe' mark for everything to go wrong now.

I was expecting the worst as I sat in the waiting room for my next ultrasound appointment. As I mindlessly scrolled through my Facebook news feed, the voice of the Channel Seven reporter broke the silence with the latest news stories. All bad, of course.

This ultrasound was the nuchal translucency scan, which screens for chromosomal abnormalities such as Down syndrome. The likelihood of a baby having one of these conditions is calculated based on a combination of factors, including the mother's age, the size of the baby, measurements of the baby's nose and neck, and a blood test that measures proteins in the placenta.

Everything in the scan itself looked perfectly fine; however, my blood test results showed that I had low levels of PAPP-A, a protein produced by the placenta.

'Based on your age and the low PAPP-A levels, there is a one in three hundred chance that the baby has Down syndrome,' Dr Smith said. 'Although the risk isn't *super* high, I'd still recommend you have a further genetic test called a non-invasive prenatal test.'

We knew that if the test showed that the baby *did* have a genetic condition, it wouldn't change what we did. Still, we wanted to be as prepared as we could be if the baby were to be born with special needs. So we decided to have the test, even though it put us $450 out of pocket.

We were thankful when the test confirmed that the baby didn't have any of the genetic conditions it had screened for. The best part was that it gave us the opportunity to find out the baby's sex. We asked the pathologist to send the results via email, and we recorded a video of ourselves as we opened them for the first time. I wore my pink dressing gown, and Geoff wore his blue dressing gown.

'Last chance to guess,' said Geoff with a smile. 'I already know it's gonna be a girl.'

'I don't know what it will be,' I said, shaking my head.

'Okay, opening up now. And the sex is... where is it?'

'It's in that PDF,' I replied, laughing. 'Apparently it's halfway down the page or something.'

It took us forever to work out how to read the results. Finally I exclaimed, 'There's two copies of the X chromosome which means it's a girl!'

'Told ya.' I'd never seen Geoff look so happy.

1 July 2018

I was conflicted about whether we should share our pregnancy on social media. I'd stood in the place of someone reading these announcements, wanting desperately for it to be me. But in the end, we shared our good news with a post on the first of July:

> *We're so excited to share that we've just signed up for the best, most challenging marathon of our lives: Parenthood! Baby Walters will be crossing the finish line in December 2018.*

Alongside the caption was a photo featuring the ultrasound image from our thirteen-week scan, a pair of bright pink Nike baby shoes, and a white onesie adorned with a 'race bib' that read *Baby Walters* with the number *1218*, signifying our baby girl's due date in December 2018.

But even as I clicked the 'Post' button, knowing we were the furthest along we'd ever been in a pregnancy, I was terrified that something could still go wrong. Every time I was in our bathroom where I'd first seen blood with the previous miscarriages, traumatic memories came surging back.

Gary was thrilled when we told him I was pregnant. Best friends with Geoff since grade four, the pair consider each other brothers.

'I'll be Uncle Gary!' he said.

'I'm so scared though,' I said.

'You'll be okay. Geoff will be there to help you out,' he joked. He assumed I feared *giving birth* to the baby.

'No, I'm scared of *not* having the baby.' I feared the guilt that would come if another baby died in my womb.

I didn't believe it was possible that I'd ever have a baby. Not even when the bleeding finally stopped around the twenty-week mark. Not even when I saw a healthy, active baby at each scan. Not even when I compared the ultrasound images and could see she was growing.

It wasn't until I felt her rolling around and moving inside me that my anxiety eased a little. Every kick, even the ones that were uncomfortable and kept me awake at night, felt like a blessing.

I was also experiencing 'diabetic burnout'. I was emotionally exhausted from striving to keep my blood glucose levels within target range twenty-four seven to ensure our baby girl stayed healthy. A 2014 study from Stanford University found that a person living with type 1 diabetes makes an extra 180 decisions each day compared to someone who doesn't live with the condition. Type 1 diabetes has its own worries before throwing pregnancy into the mix!

I remember breaking down during an appointment with my diabetes educator, Gabriela.

'I'm so over it! I just feel so hopeless. I worry that I'm hurting our baby every time my levels are high.'

'Oh, sweetie,' she said as she wrapped me in a hug. If anyone understood how I was feeling, it was Gabriela because she has type 1 diabetes herself.

If you have type 1 diabetes, I can't stress enough how important it is to have someone who supports you, whether it's your partner, parent, sibling, or a friend. Someone who is there for you through the (literal) highs and lows, both emotional and physical. Someone who sits with you to help work out why your blood glucose levels are all over the place. Someone who is willing to listen when you're going through a tough time.

For me, Geoff is my biggest supporter. He listens to me complain when my levels are high, and gets me a snack when a hypo has stolen my energy. He can handle me when I'm at 14.2 *and* when I'm at 2.8.

Geoff once put together an Excel spreadsheet to record my basal insulin patterns and changes. The formulas were too complicated for me to make any sense of, but it meant the world to know that he'd put so much time into helping me. I don't know what I'd do without him.

$$\text{\textit{Ŕ Ŕ Ŕ}}$$

3 July 2018

I started seeing a psychologist through Gidget House to help with my anxiety. Gidget House is a not-for-profit organisation that supports the emotional wellbeing of expectant and new parents. The psychologist asked me questions about my previous pregnancies, and how I was feeling about the current pregnancy.

'I've had some bleeding, and I just can't stop worrying that something is going to go wrong.'

'Are you bleeding now?'

'No, it seems to have stopped now. But with a previous pregnancy, I didn't have bleeding until I was eleven weeks pregnant, but the baby had died five weeks earlier.'

'Are you bleeding now?' she asked again.

'No.'

'So, why are you worrying?'

She made a good point! What was I worrying about? I didn't know what was going to happen in the future, but I made the decision to trust God with it. He's got everything sorted, even when we can't see it for ourselves.

CHAPTER 34

'First, we try to run faster. Then we try to run further. Then
we learn to accept ourselves and our limitations, and at last,
we can appreciate the true joy and meaning of running.'
—Amby Burfoot

BIG RED RUN
DAY 5

6 July 2014

I roll out of my sleeping bag at four and test my blood glucose level. At least I try to, but my blood glucose meter flashes an error message: *Temperature too low. Retest in a warmer location.* I put the meter in my jacket pocket to warm it up as I prepare for the second full marathon of the Big Red Run.

I want to gain an edge against my new enemy, spinifex grass, so I pull on a pair of long black and pink compression pants that cover my legs down to the ankle. I also wear my long-sleeved Big Red Run shirt to ward off the cold, but pack my short-sleeved shirt in my bag just in case it warms up during the day.

We have an earlier start time of six o'clock. The 250-kilometre Big Red Runners are tackling a gruelling eighty-four-kilometre course today, so our mandatory gear list has grown to include long-sleeved thermals and fleece.

Since we'll be starting before sunrise, with many runners expected to finish well into the night, we also need to wear fluorescent yellow vests and red flashing LED beacon lights.

Darkness envelopes us as we set off. The only thing I can see ahead of me is the illuminated strips on everyone's vests, contrasting against the pitch black. My head torch dies less than one kilometre into the course. I foolishly forgot to pack spare batteries, so I'm literally running blind over the red gibber rocks. I stumble alongside other runners to make use of their headlights.

As the first light of dawn breaks over the horizon, golden rays spill across the vast expanse of the desert. The landscape is transformed into a vibrant symphony of colours, displaying the breathtaking beauty of God's canvas.

My cheerfulness doesn't last long. I have some kind of tummy bug and feel like I'm going to throw up even before I reach the first checkpoint. Worst of all, my blood glucose shoots through the roof because I'm sick. I don't need to do a finger prick to know that I'm hyperglycaemic; I'm so thirsty, my vision is blurry, and my head is pounding.

I run straight through the first checkpoint at the 7.6-kilometre mark, not wanting the medical staff to question me. The last thing I need is a repeat of my disastrous first day. But when I reach the second checkpoint twenty kilometres into the course, I'm so nauseous that I have no choice — I have to stop.

I'm shocked to see the number 19.8 on the screen of my blood glucose meter. *Woah! How did it get* that *high?*

'I'm sorry, darling, but you'll need to stay here until your level is below 12.0,' says a middle-aged volunteer with a furrowed brow. 'Would you like me to get you some water?'

Argh, not again! I inject a few units of insulin and wait for my blood glucose level to drop. Watching the other runners breeze through the checkpoint is incredibly frustrating, but I know I need to stop stressing or it will take longer for my blood glucose to come down.

Out of the corner of my eye, I see another volunteer waving frantically at the bright yellow event helicopter, signalling for the pilot to land at the checkpoint. I'm not sure what I would do in her position, especially with limited knowledge of type 1 diabetes. But technically, I don't think she's supposed to do that. Sure, I'm sick, but I'm not dying or anything. If a runner without type 1 diabetes had a tummy bug, I doubt anyone would consider it an emergency.

I drink lots of water, both to stay hydrated and to prevent the real possibility of developing a life-threatening condition called ketoacidosis. This occurs when high levels of toxic chemical acids called ketones build up in the blood and urine. It typically happens when there is insufficient insulin in the body, and the body starts to burn fat rather than glucose for energy.

I'm not ready to give up, even as the helicopter hovers overhead. I've already ticked 'ride in a helicopter' off my bucket list; now it's time to conquer my goal of running a 150-kilometre ultramarathon. As breathtaking as the view of the Simpson Desert was from a few hundred metres up, it's nothing compared to my determination to finish the Big Red Run. There's no way I'm trading my dream for another ride.

One by one, the other runners overtake me at the checkpoint. The final group arrives and could easily fuel up and abandon me there as soon as they're ready to go. Instead, they stop to make sure I'm okay. They invite me to join them and wait patiently for the medics and volunteers to give me the all-clear to finish the next stage of the race.

And this is the moment when one of the most important lessons I've gained from running begins...

The back of the pack is where the party's at! The six other ladies and I chuckle at Mohan's jokes as we walk along the border fence dividing Queensland and South Australia. I learn that this Singaporean man has run something like 230 marathons and is known worldwide as 'Marathon Mohan'. His energy is boundless, and his smile is contagious. He whips out his camera for candid shots and blows his whistle loudly to keep us entertained.

What strikes me most about Mohan is that his drive to help fellow runners cross the finish line exceeds his own desire to reach it. Instead of concentrating on his own race time, his sole purpose is to lift the spirits of struggling runners.

As he walks beside me over the sand, he says, 'Don't run with your legs. Run with your heart and mind.'

I say 'goodbye' to my new friends at the thirty-four-kilometre checkpoint. They're all doing the 250-kilometre Big Red Run, so they have to cover double my distance today. A kind volunteer named Kyra accompanies me for the final eight kilometres.

I complete day five in 9:19:28, and I'm the final Little Red Runner to cross the finish line. If I'd known at the beginning of the day that it would take me *that* long, I would have been bitterly disappointed. But now I realise that it really doesn't matter! Who cares where you place? What truly matters is the person you are to the other runners — how you demonstrate humility, how you show your support, and how you inspire them to achieve their goals.

I call Geoff as soon as I arrive at the final campsite of the Big Red Run, which has been set up on a claypan — a dry, cracked surface of stiff, compacted clay. I tell him about the last couple of days of running, and about how much I enjoyed being at the back of the pack.

'You did it, Cheekball! Just one short jog into town to go and then you can celebrate.'

I end the call, then remember that I haven't read Geoff's note for today yet. I guess I've been having too much fun!

During race day 5 — Marathon number two (easy peasy). Darcy and Chelsea are missing you lots but hope you're doing okay and staying safe AND smashing the second marathon! Or having a beer if it's tooooo tough.

I laugh out loud when I see Geoff's drawing of two dogs saying 'woof!' I have indeed smashed day five of the Big Red Run. And with only eight kilometres to go until the ultimate finish line in Birdsville, I'm well and truly nearing the end of my outback adventure.

There's no doubt about it though — I'm going to lose at least a couple of toenails. Ahh, the sacrifices of ultrarunning…

CHAPTER 35

'Be strong and courageous. Do not be frightened, and do not be dismayed, for the LORD your God is with you wherever you go.'
—Joshua 1:9

28 – 30 August 2018

I had more bleeding at twenty-six weeks pregnant, so I booked in to see Dr Smith the following day. That same night, I received a message from Melissa:

Hey Steph, please don't freak out but I've been admitted to Dubbo Hospital for ketoacidosis. My ketones were 4.9 and I've had shortness of breath and nausea since yesterday morning. The blood test showed metabolic acidosis so it's lucky I came. My pH was 6.8 which is really low.

If I wasn't so worried about the baby, I would have booked the next flight to Dubbo. I didn't tell Melissa about the bleeding; it was the last thing she needed to be thinking about when she had her own health issues to deal with.

The following day, Dr Smith reassured me that the baby was healthy. Melissa sent another message saying that her ketones were down to 0.2 (a normal reading is lower than 0.6), and her pH was up to 7.3 (the optimum range is between 7.35 to 7.45). I breathed a huge sigh of relief when she told me she was going to be discharged the following day.

6 October 2018

Despite all the time and effort I'd put into writing checklists, buying decorations, and organising food, I questioned whether I should be going ahead with my baby shower. *What if something happens to the baby? What will I do with all the presents? Do I just give them back to everyone? Maybe I can donate them to a charity...* I didn't think I could handle having them in my house if anything were to go wrong.

On top of that, I know what it's like to go to a baby shower while struggling with fertility issues of your own. *Am I selfish if I have one?* I felt guilty for possibly putting some of my friends in a position where they'd either have to come up with an excuse not to attend or, worse, show up when it was the last place they wanted to be.

'What should I do, Cheekball?' I asked Geoff.

'It's not up to you to decide how they'll respond,' he assured me, pressing his hand on my tummy, waiting to feel the baby kick. 'Just because it might have made you sad to be invited, doesn't mean they'll feel the same.'

He was right, as usual.

So, at twenty-nine weeks pregnant, I celebrated the impending arrival of our baby girl with loved ones at Collaroy Swim Club Community Centre. I worried that it might be too early in my pregnancy to have it when I did. As it turned out, the timing could not have been better.

19 – 22 October 2018

At thirty-one weeks pregnant, I visited my GP to get a new prescription for insulin.

'How's the pregnancy going?' she asked.

'Not bad. I've had a bit of swelling in my hands and ankles, but that's normal right?' My wedding and engagement rings were now squeezing my finger, but I put it down to a common symptom of pregnancy.

'Okay, I might just check your blood pressure,' the GP said calmly. The cuff gently squeezed my right arm as it inflated.

'Hmmm… it's 150 over 100 which is quite high. I'll check it again in a few minutes. Can you do a urine sample for me in the meantime?'

I was nervous as I squatted over the toilet, peeing into a little cup. I had a history of slightly elevated blood pressure in the past, but I couldn't remember it ever being *that* high. My GP took my blood pressure measurement again when I returned to her room.

'It's 154 over 95 now. It shouldn't be higher than 140 over 90 in pregnancy. I'll just check your urine sample for protein.' She dipped a strip into my urine and compared it to a colour chart on the container.

'Your proteinuria level is 3+ which is high and shows you have damage to your kidneys. Because you have high blood pressure too, you may have a condition called pre-eclampsia.'

I'd heard that term before; Dr Smith had mentioned earlier in my pregnancy that I had an increased risk of developing it. He'd prescribed low dose aspirin to prevent the condition, which occurs in approximately twenty per cent of type 1 diabetic pregnancies.

Apart from high blood pressure and protein in my urine, there were other signs — the baby had consistently measured smaller than she should on ultrasounds, and recent blood test results showed my liver function wasn't too flash.

'You can go home and pack some things, but you need to go to the hospital today,' said my GP.

Not knowing how long I'd have to stay in the hospital, I had no idea what I should pack. *Do I pack the baby's things too?*

🏃 🏃 🏃

By the time I reached Royal North Shore Hospital, my blood pressure had risen to 172 over 98. The doctors spent the next four days trying to bring it down. They administered more and more medications, until I was on four different types! But the drugs didn't do anything.

Between the blood pressure checks every two hours, and the intermittent groans and grunts of women giving birth down the corridor, I would have been lucky to have had a total of twelve hours' sleep during my first four nights in hospital. So much for everyone's advice to 'Get as much sleep as you can before the baby arrives.'

I tried to read magazines and books to keep my mind off everything, but I found it too difficult to concentrate. Instead, I'd spend hours colouring in random pictures on a phone app called *Happy Color* (which, by the way, I only recommend if you don't have an addictive personality!).

I skimmed the pages of the world's go-to pregnancy book, *What to Expect When You're Expecting* by Heidi Murkoff. I flicked to the section on pre-eclampsia and read that, if left untreated, it could lead to serious, even fatal, complications — not only for me, but for the baby.

My medical records showed that I'd previously had an MRSA infection, however I'd never officially been 'cleared' of it. So there was a sign on the door to my room that said, *STOP. Visitors must see a nurse before entering the room.* This was followed by a precaution to put on gloves and a blue hospital gown before coming into the room.

The sign remained on my door, even after I had three nasal swabs to test for MRSA which all came back negative. It seemed like a bit of overkill; I'm sure half the nurses in the hospital had MRSA. With all the other problems I had to stress about, this was the last thing I needed.

'Are the other doctors and nurses *actually* wearing the gowns?' asked a nurse.

'Yeah, they are — the germaphobes,' Geoff laughed.

'Even the food service people don't want to come anywhere near me! They dump the trays on my table and run off with frightened looks on their faces.'

I had an ultrasound to monitor the baby's growth and to see if the pre-eclampsia had affected her. It appeared it had because she was measuring two weeks smaller than expected. This was because there was a poor blood supply to the placenta, so she wasn't getting the oxygen and nutrients she needed to develop properly.

We had a discussion with Dr Smith about the possibility of delivering the baby in the next week or so as this is the only cure for pre-eclampsia. I had injections of corticosteroids to help the baby's lungs develop before she was born. These caused my blood glucose levels to skyrocket, and I had to increase my insulin by something like 150 per cent to avoid hyperglycaemia.

I heard the cries of newborn babies outside my room, and prayed that I'd one day hear that of our own baby girl. But not yet; she was still too little and needed to do a bit more growing.

However, by the evening of the twenty-second of October, my blood pressure had risen to 195 over 108. Doctor Google told me if the top number went over two hundred, there was a high risk of seizures, brain damage, and stroke. The air around me felt thin and suffocating as I began to hyperventilate.

I was admitted to the maternity ward where I was injected with magnesium sulfate, a medication that helps to prevent seizures.

'Has your vision changed at all?' Dr Smith asked.

'No,' I replied.

But within hours, I realised the room around me was out of focus and flashes of light danced before me. I also felt pressure behind my left eye and an intense headache that didn't go away after taking pain killers. When I told Dr Smith, he scheduled an emergency caesarean section for the following day.

CHAPTER 36

*'Every good and perfect gift is from above, coming
down from the Father of the heavenly lights, who
does not change like shifting shadows.'*
—James 1:17 (NIV)

23 October 2018

At just thirty-one weeks and five days pregnant, I was wheeled into an operating theatre where I'd meet my baby girl for the first time. My whole body started shaking when the anaesthetist injected the epidural into my lower back. It was difficult to talk because my teeth were chattering so much. I tried to stay calm but failed miserably.

Geoff filmed me as I lay on the bed, about to be sliced open by Dr Smith.

'Do you have any thoughts, Cheekball?' he asked.

'No, no thoughts.' Yeah, right! My brain was in overdrive.

'How are you feeling?'

'I don't know. It's weird.' A blue curtain separated us from Dr Smith and the baby. I felt strange pulling sensations and pressure, but no pain at all.

It was only two minutes into the operation when Dr Smith announced, 'The baby's coming out shortly.' I nodded, too nervous to speak.

'I've got something to show you,' he said, as a nurse pulled down the blue curtain.

'Oh, wow!' Geoff exclaimed.

There she was — a perfect baby girl. *Our* perfect baby girl. She reached her thin arms up into the air as if to say, 'Hello, world. Here I am.' Tears welled in my eyes when I heard her cry for the first time.

'Congratulations! She's a beautiful baby,' smiled Dr Smith. 'I'm just lowering her down to get as much blood flow from the cord and placenta as we can.'

We'd opted for delayed cord clamping, which means the umbilical cord isn't immediately clamped and cut. Instead, it remains attached for an extra minute or so which has many health benefits for the baby.

'She's weeing on me! She's just like her mother — giving me a hard time already,' joked Dr Smith.

'How do you feel now, Cheekball?' Geoff asked.

'Happy.' No other word more perfectly describes how I felt at that moment.

We named our daughter Mariella in honour of four of the most import-ant women in my life: my mum Maria, my twin sister Melissa, Geoff's mum Marcelle, and my best friend Aurelle. Mariella is a mix of each of their names, as well as my middle name, Marie. We also connected with the name's meaning, *wished-for child*, because we'd longed for a baby for so long.

Geoff followed Dr Smith as he carried Mariella over to the other side of the operating theatre. She weighed a teeny tiny 1.305 kilograms and measured forty-one centimetres long. I'd been convinced I'd have a big baby because women with type 1 diabetes usually do! I'd asked my friends and family not to buy any newborn-sized 0000 clothing, thinking she'd go straight into a size 000. Little did I know she'd be too small even for 000000 clothing!

The nurses rushed her to the neonatal intensive care unit (NICU) just minutes after she was born. Watching Mariella from a distance, unable to hold her, felt completely surreal.

While I recovered from the caesarean section in my hospital bed, I video-called Geoff who was with Mariella in the NICU. He told me her initial blood glucose reading was 1.9. A normal level for a newborn baby is 2.6 or above, but babies born to women with type 1 diabetes have a higher chance of hypoglycaemia. Thankfully, her blood glucose levels quickly stabilised with the breast milk I'd expressed before she was born.

Because of my own history with MRSA, Mariella was placed in an isolation room. This was a blessing in disguise because there was a nurse looking after her one-on-one around the clock. Mariella was put on a continuous positive airway pressure (CPAP) machine because she needed a bit of help to breathe.

However, unlike many premature babies, she only needed this for forty-eight hours. Apart from mild jaundice, which was treated overnight with a treatment called phototherapy, she had no other medical issues.

Mariella was born at 1:48 pm; the first time I held her was 8:57 pm. The CPAP machine gurgled softly in the background as Geoff helped me into a reclining chair. A nurse carefully placed Mariella on my bare chest so we could lay skin-to-skin. After years of heartache, holding my baby girl brought me unimaginable hope and healing. I prayed, *Thank you for this perfect gift, Lord!*

I gently stroked Mariella's soft olive cheek as she wrapped her petite hand around my index finger. An oxygen mask smothered her face, but I could just make out her cute little button nose. I felt the gentle rise and fall of her chest on my own. Without question, Mariella is a miracle.

30 October – 6 December 2018

I was discharged from Royal North Shore a week after Mariella was born. Leaving her at the hospital in the hands of complete strangers felt unnatural. *Can I trust them to look after our baby?* The only thing stopping us from bringing her home was the fact that she was so little.

I thought about the *Rugrats* episode where baby Tommy says, 'I remember the first time I saw my mom. I think I was in a fish tank or something. It seemed like nobody knowed I was there, and it was scary. Then my mom came. I don't even think I even knowed she was my mom then, but when she held my hand I didn't feel scared no more. As long as I was there, she never let go.'

It broke my heart wondering if Mariella was scared when Geoff and I left the hospital at the end of each day. I set three-hourly alarms overnight to express milk, ready for the nurses to feed her when I'd have to say goodbye again the next night. I'd prop myself up in bed, sleepily scrolling through the photos I'd taken of Mariella. My breast pump hummed rhythmically in the background as I studied her perfect features, yearning for the day we'd bring her home.

Geoff lost his job at a prestigious accounting firm in North Sydney a week before I was admitted to hospital with pre-eclampsia. He arrived home early one afternoon, which was so unusual for him given the long hours he'd been working. He was holding a box full of Sultana Bran, muesli bars, and other snacks he'd been storing in his work drawers, so I guessed immediately what had happened.

'Um, did you lose your job, Cheekball?'

'How did you guess?'

This was another blessing in disguise. Geoff was there with me through everything, from when I first entered the emergency room, until the day Mariella was finally ready to come home with us six weeks later. Once again, God's timing couldn't have been better.

CHAPTER 37

*'Running is not, as it so often seems, only about what you did
in your last race or about how many miles you ran last week.
It is, in a much more important way, about community, about
appreciating all the miles run by other runners, too.'*
—Richard O'Brien

10 December 2018

I had a check-up with Dr Smith when Mariella was seven weeks old. The
first question I asked him was, 'When can I start running again?'

'You can run now!'

I was so surprised to hear him say that because I'd read somewhere that
I had to wait until twelve weeks post-caesarean section. I admit I didn't get
straight back into running. However, I did join Running Mums Australia,
a network for Australian women to connect and discuss all things running.

Geoff and I invested in a Baby Jogger City Elite pram, inspired by glow-
ing reviews I read on the Running Mums Facebook group. Health pro-
fessionals advise against running with an infant before they're at least six
months of age. I couldn't wait to take Mariella on her first run when she
was old enough, and hoped she'd one day share my passion for it.

12 March – 30 April 2019

In March 2019, Geoff and I moved with four-month-old Mariella to Queensland's capital city, Brisbane. Geoff wasted no time in lacing up his running shoes. He mapped out a five-kilometre course through our estate's labyrinth of streets.

I made my return to running six weeks later, when Mariella was six months old. I set out with no grand expectations about pace or distance. But I astonished myself and somehow managed to run the entire five kilometres without stopping, clocking a respectable enough time of 36:19.

I enjoyed my new routine of running with Mariella in the pram, sneaking in a workout while she napped peacefully. Yet it was no easy task! A 2012 study in the *Journal of Sports Medicine and Physical Fitness* found that running with a pram results in a significantly higher heart rate, perceived level of exertion, and lactate concentration.

Running with a little human also requires a great deal of planning. You need to time the run perfectly to suit their schedule. You need to pack more snacks and toys than you think they'll possibly want. You need to choose a route that won't take you too far from home. And you need to make sure the terrain is suitable for a pram. It's a logistical feat, but the rewards far outweigh the effort.

4 May 2019

For many years, Geoff and I kept hearing about a global phenomenon known as 'parkrun'. Everyone we met who was involved with parkrun was shouting about it from the rooftops. The concept is simple: turn up each

Saturday morning at one of over two thousand parkrun locations around the world, and walk, jog, or run a five-kilometre course. Everyone who registers has their own barcode to record their times.

We decided to check out our local parkrun in Augustine Heights. I'd formed the idea that only fast runners could take part, so I told Geoff, 'I'll just wait at the finish line with the baby.'

'Come on, Cheekball. You can just take it easy.'

'No, I won't be fast enough,' I insisted.

I had flashbacks to my last place finish in the hundred-metre sprint in primary school. Even though I didn't know anyone else there, I was worried that I'd embarrass myself if I was too slow.

When the Run Director sent the parkrunners on their way at seven o'clock sharp, Geoff took off running. I found myself swept up in a crowd of keen runners, and I was taking part in my first parkrun!

A volunteer marshal didn't realise Geoff and I were newbies, so she didn't direct us the right way. We ended up running five and a half kilometres instead of the usual five! She must have assumed we were regulars who already knew the course. Thus, our parkrun journey began, and we've loved it ever since.

One of the things I love about parkrun is that it's so incredibly inclusive. It doesn't matter if you're a walker taking your first steps into a healthy lifestyle, or an elite athlete training for the next Olympic Games. Everyone is welcome, no matter how fast or slow they finish the course. Not to mention it's completely free!

What keeps people coming back week after week is the real community spirit that drives parkrun. Each event is organised by dedicated volunteers who generously give up their Saturday morning sleep-in to set markers around the course, scan barcodes to record runners' times, or stick to the back of the pack as tailwalkers. The magic that is parkrun simply wouldn't be possible without the incredible support of these 'hi-vis heroes', as they're fondly called.

By the way, you haven't come across a typo in a professional editor's own book; parkrun is intentionally written as one word with a lower case 'p', representing its simplicity and inclusivity. I couldn't agree more with Tim Oberg, the legend who brought parkrun to Australia back in April 2011, when he said, 'People want a place to belong, a place to meet friends, a place to get away from their digital lives, and parkrun offers that.'

Saturday has become my favourite day of the week. It can be oh so tempting to stay in bed — especially when it's bitterly cold, or your baby has woken up multiple times during the night — but I can't say I've ever regretted getting up to go to parkrun. It's the perfect chance to get away from the chaos of everyday life, and simply enjoy time with the ones you love while getting fit in the fresh air. And let's not forget the delicious café brunch afterwards! What better way to spend a Saturday morning?

🏃 🏃 🏃

21 – 28 December 2019

I set myself a goal to run five kilometres in under twenty-five minutes before Christmas Day 2019. My previous personal best was 25:06 — that was the first five kilometres of the 2017 Sydney Morning Herald Half Marathon when I was at my peak. So I knew this wouldn't be a simple undertaking.

On the twenty-first of December, just a few days before Christmas, Geoff, Mariella and I visited Kirra parkrun in the Gold Coast suburb of Coolangatta. Kirra parkrun is renowned for its flat, fast course running parallel to the beach, and attracts runners from near and far looking for their next five-kilometre personal best.

Occasionally at parkrun, there are volunteer pacers who help people achieve their goal times. On this particular Saturday, there was a twenty-five-minute pacer named Darrell, who ran alongside me the entire way. He motivated me to keep my pace under five minutes per kilometre for the entire time.

'That's it! Keep going! Just visualise crossing that finish line.'

Every part of my body burned when I finally reached it. I forgot to stop my Garmin, only remembering to press the button when I was well past the timekeeper. The screen displayed *25:03. Oh no! Did I just miss my goal?* It was an agonising wait for the official parkrun result to show up in my inbox. I couldn't believe it when I read the words: *Your time was 00:24:52.*

'Cheekball!' I called out to Geoff who was pushing Mariella on a swing. 'I did it! I ran five kilometres in under twenty-five minutes!'

'Congratulations, Cheekball! I knew you could do it.'

On the twenty-eighth of December, when we were in Sydney visiting family for the Christmas break, we visited Chipping Norton parkrun. I noticed early on that there were no other females ahead of me. I figured it wouldn't stay that way for long, but I surged forward and managed to hold my lead, placing first female, and fifteenth overall!

Okay, so there were only fifty-eight parkrunners in total there, and my time was nothing special at 26:08. But I knew something like this was unlikely to ever happen again, so I celebrated the victory for all its worth.

CHAPTER 38

'Why couldn't Pheidippides have died here?'
—Frank Shorter's comment to Kenny Moore at the
thirty-five-kilometre mark of his first marathon

12 January 2020

I competed in three short distance races with Mariella in tow in 2019. The first race was the 5.7-kilometre fun run at the Gold Coast Marathon in July, where I rugged up Mariella in a fluffy llama onesie. I took my time, soaking in the warmth of the sun on my back and the joy of sharing this moment with my little one.

The second race was the five-kilometre Bridge to Brisbane in August. I dressed up as a stormtrooper, while Mariella looked adorable in her ewok costume. I'd converted our pram into a TIE fighter spacecraft from the *Star Wars* films. Passersby would have found it amusing to see a stormtrooper breastfeeding an ewok! I was drenched in sweat, and my insulin pump had gradually slid its way down the inside of my costume from my hip to my calf over the final few kilometres.

The third race was the five-kilometre DC Batman Run in September. I dressed up as Super Girl and Mariella was Robin. We raced our 'Batmobile' pram from Turbot Street in Brisbane's central business district, running alongside the brown waters of Brisbane River, before reaching the pedestrian and cyclist-friendly Goodwill Bridge in South Bank.

The 2020 Cadbury Marathon would be my first solo race since having Mariella. I usually drift off to sleep without a problem, but the night before a race is always different as the anticipation of what lies ahead races through my mind. Add to that the sleep deprivation that comes with being a new mum, and I wasn't exactly feeling fresh when race morning arrived.

Known as the 'Chocolate Run', the Cadbury Marathon starts and finishes at the iconic Cadbury Chocolate Factory in Claremont, Tasmania. I arrived at the race village much later than I'd planned. I was still pinning my race bib on my singlet as I made my way through the crowd to the four-hour pacers. I ran out of time to apply sunscreen after waiting forever in the long Portaloo line. This would prove to be an epic fail considering Tasmania's extreme ultraviolet levels.

The course consisted of two laps of bitumen that snaked along the River Derwent. One of the highlights was running across Bowen Bridge at the halfway point, with an outlook towards the city of Hobart which lay nestled beneath majestic Mount Wellington.

I tried to remember to smile because I'd read in *Runner's World* magazine that runners who smile use less oxygen, run more economically, and have a lower perceived rate of exertion than those who frown. I also had a goal to get a decent professional race photo of myself for a change. I truly believe this is one of the most difficult things I've ever attempted, quite possibly on par with actually running a marathon.

It's impossible for me to look good while I'm running. The race photographer always catches me off guard, snapping unexpected shots as I drag myself over the crest of an outrageously steep incline, my face contorted in a forced half-smile as I pretend I'm loving life when, in reality, I feel like I'm about to die.

At other times, I can see there's a photographer up ahead and I try to think of a fun pose, but I can never quite find the energy to pull it off. Usually all I'm concerned about in that moment is getting to the finish line alive. Still, I held out hope of achieving a perfect photo during this race.

I'd never been more consistent with my training than I was in the lead up to the Cadbury Marathon. I'd put pressure on myself to achieve my dream of finally running a sub four-hour marathon — the goal time that had eluded me at the 2017 Gold Coast Marathon. So I was miserable when I lost the pacers about twenty-five kilometres into the race. I simply *could not* move my legs fast enough to keep up with them.

God often speaks to me through music. In this moment of need, I prayed that He would give me a song, and Lauren Daigle's 'You Say' filled my Shokz headphones. The uplifting lyrics were a powerful reminder that I am loved, I am strong, and I am valued, even when I believe the opposite.

God showed me that I'd been placing so much of my self-worth in my own abilities — not just as a runner, but as a wife and mum. I was still comparing myself to others, echoing the same insecurities I'd felt growing up with Melissa. I was listening to the voices in my head that insisted that I'd never be good enough.

But God reminded me that how He saw me had absolutely *nothing* to do with my performance in the race. It didn't matter if I finished in under four hours or not. What truly mattered was my identity in Him — understanding who He is, and who He created me to be.

Although I didn't run a sub four-hour marathon, I was so happy to achieve a new personal best time of 4:04:44 on a tough course. For the entire race, I'd been visualising the chocolate promised by the race organisers as a reward for crossing the finish line.

I couldn't believe it; I got the exact same amount that Geoff did even though he'd only run the five-kilometre race! Not only that, but one of the two chocolate bars in my goodie bag was a Picnic which I don't even like, so I ended up giving that to Geoff too! In fairness, Geoff's race was on a grass course, and he was pushing Mariella in the pram, but still…

Nonetheless, I was overwhelmed with gratitude as I sat in the shade of a tree on the Cadbury Chocolate Factory's manicured lawn. Beautiful fourteen-month-old Mariella bounced up and down on my lap, staring wide-eyed at Freddo Frog and Caramello Koala in the distance. Even my new unevenly tanned thighs and shoulders couldn't take away from my contentment.

🏃 🏃 🏃

As I perused the gallery of my race photos later that week, I was thrilled to see how close I'd come to attaining that perfect running photo. There was a half decent shot of me in my Running Mums Australia singlet and brightly coloured Disney shorts featuring Mickey, Minnie, Donald, and Daisy. I was grinning from ear to ear because I was so close to the end.

But why did my hair have to be so frizzy?! Oh well. I'll keep striving to get that perfect race photo.

CHAPTER 39

'Faith is a journey with many steep hills.'
—Bear Grylls

April – September 2020

As the Covid-19 pandemic swept the globe, hardworking individuals battled to make ends meet as their incomes dwindled, and toilet paper and tinned foods disappeared from supermarket shelves. Meanwhile, runners in lockdown were forced to get creative, completing the marathons they'd diligently trained for on their balconies.

But not everything about 2020 was terrible. In April, shortly after Australia shut its international borders to stop the spread of the virus, I fell pregnant again.

With the border closed between Queensland and New South Wales, we couldn't share the good news with our family in person. So I ordered a shirt online that said *Promoted to Big Sister*, which Mariella wore during one of our weekly family video calls.

After what felt like an eternity due to poor Internet connectivity that made our video blurry, everyone was finally able to read the shirt. They congratulated us from their homes over nine hundred kilometres away.

Geoff and I announced our pregnancy on Facebook on the first of July, exactly two years to the day that we announced our pregnancy with

Mariella. My passion for LEGO had grown exponentially during the pandemic, so I posted a photo of a 'LEGO set' with the number *120121*, representing our baby's due date of the twelfth of January 2021. It had LEGO minifigures depicting Geoff and Mariella, plus me pushing a baby in a pram, with the caption, *God's building our family.*

At my twenty-week scan, Geoff and I were delighted when we found out we were having another daughter. We both loved the name Hannah, which means *grace* in Hebrew, but I wondered if we should choose another unique name like we had with Mariella.

A friend suggested we use Kinder, an app where you swipe right on baby names you like, and swipe left on ones you don't like. You receive 'matches' on the names you've both swiped right on.

I was lying in bed next to Geoff one afternoon, quickly flicking through the names on the app.

'Oh man, I don't like any of these names!' I said.

'Why don't we just go with Hannah?' Geoff asked.

At that exact moment, the name *Hannah* appeared on my screen! And that settled the matter; our new baby girl's name would be Hannah.

Most of my prenatal checkups were conducted via Zoom video calls. Due to the strict Covid restrictions in place at Mater Mothers' Hospital in South Brisbane, I had to attend all the face-to-face appointments on my own — wearing a face mask, of course. It was far from ideal that I had to leave Mariella with Geoff during work hours so often.

I read news stories of women around the world whose partners weren't allowed to be in the birthing suite with them. *What if I go into labour and Geoff can't be there with me?* This was my biggest fear as I approached my due date; I think I was more scared about Geoff not being there than I was about the labour itself!

18 – 19 September 2020

Just like my previous pregnancies, this one was one heck of a roller coaster. I had no energy during the first trimester as I experienced one hypo after another. In the final trimester, at seventy-four kilograms (fourteen kilograms heavier than my pre-pregnancy weight), I could barely get out of bed due to severe lower back pain. *How did I ever run five-kilometre parkruns, let alone ultramarathons?*

By twenty-three weeks pregnant, I'd well and truly hit insulin resistance. From the second trimester, pregnant women with type 1 diabetes will find that the amount of insulin they need to manage their blood glucose levels increases, sometimes *three times* as much as prior to pregnancy. This is because the hormones produced by the placenta cause insulin to become less effective.

I'd been struggling to stay in target range for a week or so, and the last thing I needed was to get sick with a tummy bug. I couldn't keep anything down, not even water. I lay on the couch for an entire day with a bucket at the ready. My head was throbbing with the worst migraine I'd ever experienced.

'What's wrong, Mummy?' Mariella asked, staring at me with her big, brown eyes.

It didn't dawn on me until that evening that perhaps I didn't have a tummy bug at all. *What if I have high ketones?* It would explain the stomach pain, vomiting, and migraine.

I sent Geoff out to buy a box of ketone test strips from the pharmacy. After peeing on the strip, my fear was realised when I compared it against the colour chart. The dark purple indicated there were indeed high ketones in my urine.

I went straight to the pregnancy assessment unit at Mater Mothers' Hospital. As I sat in the waiting room, I began to worry that Hannah wasn't as active as she usually was. Geoff had to sit in a different waiting room due to the hospital's Covid policy, so I was alone with Doctor Google. I read that ketones can cross the placenta and damage the baby's brain. *Please protect her, Lord*, I prayed.

When I was finally seen by a nurse, my ketones were 2.3, which meant I was at risk of developing ketoacidosis. I was hooked up to a saline drip to help flush my body of the ketones, as well as a glucose drip to boost my energy because I'd been unable to eat for over twenty-four hours.

Thankfully, it worked, and my ketones eventually dropped to 0.1. I was beyond relieved when I was discharged the following day. I couldn't wait to get home and give Mariella a cuddle.

29 – 30 December 2020

Women with type 1 diabetes are five times more likely to suffer stillbirths. Because glucose crosses the placenta, the baby's blood glucose levels reflect the mother's. If they're high, the baby will produce extra insulin for themselves. The combination of extra glucose and extra insulin can make the baby grow too big. For this reason, I was booked in to have an induction of labour at thirty-eight weeks.

I was determined to do everything in my power to go into labour before the induction date. I'd read that an induced labour can be more painful than a natural one. Rather than building up slowly like in natural labour, contractions can start more quickly and be stronger in induced labour.

So I followed Doctor Google's advice and went for long walks, enjoyed plenty of sex, and ate the spiciest Indian food my taste buds could handle. But none of it worked; I was admitted to hospital as scheduled.

At seven thirty pm on the thirtieth of December, twenty-two hours after I had two balloon catheters inserted, and six hours after a midwife broke my waters, our beautiful Hannah entered this crazy world.

Without going into too much detail, let's just say that giving birth to a 4.044-kilogram baby without any pain relief was tougher than my five marathons and four ultramarathons combined. That first shower after the birth was the best shower of my life — even better than the one I had after six days of not showering during the Big Red Run.

Despite my fear that I couldn't possibly love Hannah as much as I love Mariella, I fell head over heels for her instantly. She was super alert, with chubby cheeks, and a cute button nose like her big sister's. She was also incredibly strong, holding her head up on her own from the moment the midwife placed her on my chest. Just like Hannah in the Bible, my heart rejoiced in the Lord for blessing us with this precious child (1 Samuel 2:1).

31 December 2020

On New Year's Eve, when Hannah was one day old, Geoff brought Mariella to the hospital to meet her new baby sister.

'Baby! Sweeping!' Mariella said over and over as she watched Hannah sleep.

Hannah was wrapped in the distinctive pink, blue, yellow, and white striped blanket that most babies born in an Australian hospital are photographed in.

'Gentle on her head,' Geoff smiled, as Mariella gripped the side of Hannah's head.

'Head!' Mariella exclaimed, pointing at her own. 'Nose!' Hannah scrunched up her face as Mariella poked her in the nose, before Mariella gave her a few soft kisses on the cheek.

Their first interaction would have melted the heart of anyone who witnessed it. What a perfect way to end an imperfect year.

8 January 2021

Unlike my pregnancy with Mariella, I didn't develop pre-eclampsia while I was pregnant with Hannah. However, as I recovered in hospital after the birth, I did have some high blood pressure readings.

'You're fine to leave,' said my doctor, 'but it looks like you may have postpartum hypertension. Make sure you keep an eye on your blood pressure when you're back home.'

On the eighth of January, five days after bringing Hannah home, my blood pressure was still high, the vision in my right eye was blurry, and I had an intense headache that Panadol had no effect on whatsoever.

I returned to the hospital. The nurse remained silent as the cuff around my arm slowly deflated.

'Is it still high?' I asked.

'Yes, but I'll check it again in a few minutes.'

A few minutes later, she inflated the cuff again. Without a word, the nurse walked to the other side of the room and pressed a button which sounded a code blue emergency alert.

My whole life flashed before my eyes when she said, 'Please try not to worry, but your blood pressure is 204 over 120.' Within seconds, three doctors and two more nurses came running into the room. *Um, how exactly does she expect me not to panic?!*

'Please tell my family I love them,' I said to Geoff, fighting back the tears. 'Should I write letters to the girls, so they have something to remember me by?'

I was amazed at how *calm* Geoff seemed. He said he wasn't worried because he sensed it wasn't my time yet. I, on the other hand, was freaking out!

But, as usual, Geoff was right — it wasn't my time. The doctors injected me with magnesium sulfate to prevent a seizure. I took multiple medications to lower my blood pressure. Within a week, my readings had returned to normal. God had once again saved my life, and I was determined to never take it for granted again.

CHAPTER 40

*'I didn't go to religion to make me happy. I always knew a bottle
of Port would do that. If you want a religion to make you feel
really comfortable, I certainly don't recommend Christianity.'*
—C.S. Lewis

27 July 2021 – 2 July 2022

The road to the 2022 Gold Coast Marathon was far from smooth. However, as most marathoners will attest, the training — rather than the race itself — is the real challenge.

When Hannah was seven months old, Geoff and I signed up for the Couch to 5K app — a virtual fitness program that transforms you from couch potato to five-kilometre runner. Every muscle of my body protested after my fifteen-month hiatus from running. But the program worked, and I was back to running five kilometres non-stop by the end of September.

I still had my goal to run a sub four-hour marathon, and was determined to give it another crack at the Gold Coast Marathon. For the first time since becoming a runner in 2011, I enlisted the help of a running coach.

Pat Carroll, himself a four-time winner of the Gold Coast Marathon with a personal best time of 2:09:39, is a legend on the Australian running scene. Since retiring from the elite level, Pat has assisted over three thousand people to achieve their running goals through his online coaching program.

This was an absolute game changer! Pat wasn't afraid to tell me what I needed to hear, and he pushed me well outside my comfort zone. Knowing that I needed to report back to him with updates about my training kept me motivated to stay on track.

I ran one-kilometre laps around the streets near our house well into the night, my limited night vision causing me to narrowly miss trampling on repulsive cane toads. I ran despite the devastating floods that inundated Brisbane in February, mixing up my usual routes to prevent soggy feet.

I wrestled with mum guilt. *Am I selfish for spending so much time running instead of being with the girls?* As any running mum will tell you, it's a challenge to juggle motherhood with training for a marathon, or any race distance for that matter. It can be difficult to know what to prioritise when there's so much that needs to be done — cleaning, cooking, changing nappies (okay, that last one's a non-negotiable!).

Sure, I could have set out at four in the morning to finish my run before they woke up, but they're both such early risers, and I'm not exactly a morning person! Instead, Geoff and I would squeeze in our long runs while the girls were at daycare, or we'd load them into the pram and jog to a playground, where we could do laps and take turns pushing them on the swings.

My perspective on this has changed in recent times. I now recognise that running is a tool that helps me be a *better* mum. Not only does it make me less cranky, but it also serves as a powerful example for my daughters about the importance of leading a healthy, active lifestyle.

I hope my commitment to running will teach them valuable lessons about perseverance and the significance of hard work in achieving their goals — not just in running, but in all aspects of life.

29 March 2022

On the twenty-ninth of March 2022, I took my last sip of alcohol. In the year or so leading up to this date, I found myself drinking almost every day. And the amount I consumed was slowly but steadily increasing, until I was drinking close to a bottle and a half of wine some days.

I'd pour my first glass as early as eleven in the morning, desperate for relief from the many stressors of life. I drank to cope with the demands of being a stay-at-home mum. I felt pressure to be productive, yet I barely had time to shower, let alone do housework. My life revolved around the girls, and although they brought me so much joy every single day, they were — and still are! — hard work. Living ten hours' drive from family in Sydney meant that alcohol became my support system.

I'd lost my sense of identity. *Who am I besides being a mum? What is my purpose in life?* Everything I did seemed so meaningless. It wasn't, of course. As Graeme McLean said to me long before I had children, 'Motherhood will be the most challenging, yet the most rewarding thing you'll ever do in your life.' But in my sleep deprived state, I couldn't see that the season I was in was one to be cherished, not resented.

I feel vulnerable sharing this part of my story, perhaps more so than anything else I've shared in this memoir. But the truth is that every one of us struggles with sin, and Christians are not immune. I was leading a double life — attending church hungover on Sunday morning after getting drunk on Saturday night.

Why do I keep doing this, God? What's wrong with me? I resonated with Paul's words in Romans 7:15: 'I do not understand what I do. For what I want to do I do not do, but what I hate I do.'

I foolishly believed I could control my addiction, forgetting 1 Corinthians 10:12 which says, 'Let anyone who thinks that he stands take heed lest he fall.' I tried and failed to restrict myself to one or two drinks each night. I asked Geoff to keep me accountable, while secretly hiding how much I was really drinking. He was worried about me, but he knew he couldn't force me to change; it needed to be my decision.

During an evening run, suffering with a terrible headache after another day of drinking, and feeling ashamed that I wasn't the wife or mother I knew God wanted me to be, I decided that something needed to change.

I listened to the audiobook, *This Naked Mind: Control Alcohol, Find Freedom, Discover Happiness & Change Your Life* by Annie Grace. Annie's personal story completely transformed my perspective on alcohol. It helped me to see that rather than *solving* my depression and anxiety, alcohol was in fact *causing* it. And learning about its potential impact on my physical health terrified me.

I came to the realisation that I had no reason to drink alcohol, and every reason to avoid it. It did absolutely nothing to help me, and only caused harm — not only to me, but to those closest to me, especially Geoff and the girls.

Jamaican sprinter Usain Bolt is known as the 'Fastest Man Alive'. In 2009, he broke his own world record in the hundred-metre sprint, completing the distance in a blistering time of 9.58 seconds. The current marathon world record stands at a phenomenal two hours and thirty-five seconds, set by Kenyan runner Kelvin Kiptum during the 2023 Chicago Marathon, just four months before his untimely death in a tragic road accident.

Usain and Kelvin's training schedules would have been miles apart. The hundred-metre sprint and the marathon are completely different events, requiring different physical preparation and mental strategies. In a sprint, you need a quick burst of energy over a short distance and time. In a marathon, you must keep a steady pace over a longer period to ensure you last the entire 42.195 kilometres.

If you train for a hundred-metre sprint when in fact you've signed up for a marathon, there's no way you'll succeed. A few kilometres in, negative thoughts will enter your mind, and you'll want to throw in the towel.

In the same way, the Christian life is a marathon, not a sprint. It's a test of endurance, requiring discipline to go the distance. What this looks like in my life is that I've made a commitment to abstain from alcohol indefinitely, to 'throw off everything that hinders and the sin that so easily entangles' (Hebrews 12:1). While I don't necessarily think all Christians should steer clear of alcohol, I believe it's the right choice for me.

I understand that battling alcohol addiction may be a lifelong journey, but I have this assurance in 1 Corinthians 10:13: 'No temptation has overtaken you that is not common to man. God is faithful, and he will not let you be tempted beyond your ability, but with the temptation he will also provide the way of escape, that you may be able to endure it.'

With this promise in mind, I'm grateful that Jesus has already triumphed over my sin through His sacrifice on the cross. I trust Him to guide me as my Pacer on this marathon called 'life', confident that I will share in His victory when He carries me across the ultimate finish line.

CHAPTER 41

'If one could run without getting tired, I don't think
one would often want to do anything else.'
—C.S. Lewis

5 – 14 June 2022

Four weeks before the Gold Coast Marathon, Covid-19 struck the Walters
family. I'd been following news reports on the rising case numbers in Australia,
knowing it was only a matter of time before we caught it too. Our symptoms
were relatively mild, but I was concerned that the virus would reverse all the
hard work that Geoff and I had put into training for the marathon.

We took a week off running. This wasn't by choice; the Queensland
Government had made home isolation mandatory for seven days after testing positive for Covid-19, and we didn't own a treadmill. Thankfully, we
didn't lose too much fitness, and we were able to continue with Pat's scheduled program in the final few weeks before the event.

I later learned that doctors recommend a slow return to exercise following Covid-19 because heart and lung damage can occur even after mild illness. They advise that runners should wait until they've had no symptoms
for at least seven days. *Oops.*

3 July 2022

The morning of the marathon arrived. After a frantic dash to catch our Uber, Geoff and I arrived at the race village at five o'clock. This gave us an hour to fit in a pre-race coffee and visit to the Portaloos. I was buzzing with anticipation as we walked over to the four-hour pacers.

'Oh, do you have type 1 diabetes?' a woman in her twenties asked. 'Me too!' Her eyes sparked with recognition as she lifted her arm, proudly revealing her continuous glucose monitor, mirroring the one on my own. Meeting other runners who, like me, refuse to let type 1 diabetes hold them back from chasing their goals always boosts my spirits. It's as if I've made an instant friend.

I tossed my well-worn grey hoodie over the heads of the other runners, adding it to the pile of clothing discarded as donations to charity. The starting gun fired, and we were off. We barely made it two kilometres before Geoff uttered the words I'd been dreading to hear him say: 'I have to go to the toilet.'

Apparently carb loading doesn't agree with Geoff. He'd spent a long time on the loo the previous day, and this morning was no different. He'd already been to the toilet twice before the race even started, and needed to go not once, not twice, but *three* times during the race!

Despite developing what I was sure would be a foolproof sub four-hour marathon strategy, our race just didn't go to plan. We'd hoped to only walk when we needed to take a drink break. This is because drinking from a paper cup while running is a tricky thing to master, and I can't stand it when sticky electrolytes spill onto my hands and legs. But Geoff had an absolute shocker of a day and couldn't keep up with me! I lost count of how many times I stopped to wait for him on the side of the road.

However, as important as my sub four-hour goal was to me, I wasn't going to leave Geoff behind. He'd given me constant support for the past eleven months, jogging all our training runs at my pace, and encouraging me to get out the door when it was the last thing I felt like doing. We were in this race together.

I hit my own wall at the halfway mark. I'd developed two blisters: one on my left big toe, and the other on the sole of my left foot. *Ouch! Did I just lose a toenail?* I appreciated the encouraging words from other women in the Running Mums Australia community along the way, who pushed me to keep going when I was at my worst.

Geoff and I simultaneously turned on the Spotify playlist we'd carefully curated to inspire us to put one foot in front of the other. It worked; I got over the wall much quicker than I have in previous marathons. In fact, I felt like I was soaring through the clouds for much of the race.

'C'mon, Cheekballs! Looking strong!' shouted our friend Rob from the sidelines.

My Garmin vibrated to let me know I'd reached the thirty-two-kilometre mark. *Easy — just two parkruns to go.* I find it mentally easier to break down long races into smaller segments, focusing on one section at a time rather than looking at the distance as a whole.

The finish line came into view as I rounded the final bend. I realised that Geoff had once again fallen behind. I felt like a bit of an idiot when I stopped a few metres before the line, but there was no way I was going to cross it without him by my side. I ran back about a hundred metres to meet him, and we finished together in the official time of 4:31:21.

If it hadn't been for all of Geoff's toilet stops and having to slow down for him to catch up with me, then I honestly think I could have broken four hours. Although it was so far from the time I'd hoped for, I can't explain in words the sheer bliss I felt at that moment. I learned the important lesson that not every race has to be about getting a new personal best time. Sometimes it's about helping someone else cross the finish line.

Anyway, there's always another marathon to sign up for...

🏃 🏃 🏃

I stretched my stiff muscles under the shade of a tree as I watched the other finishers shuffle around. They wore their race medals with pride as they drank their takeaway coffees. I was so grateful to Rob for waiting in a ridiculously long café queue to get one for me. He was also there to chase after the girls because I could barely walk, let alone run!

Geoff's dad John had looked after Mariella and Hannah while we ran the marathon. Because we'd been in such a hurry to get to the start line that morning, we ran out of time to explain everything he needed to know. John had called Geoff a couple of times during the race when he had questions.

'Mariella won't let me put a nappy on her. What should I do?' he'd asked.

'No, Dad, she doesn't wear a nappy. She's toilet trained now,' replied Geoff.

John did an exceptional job caring for two energetic little girls on his own for over six hours! Even still, I couldn't help but laugh when I first saw the girls after the race. Hannah had honey smeared all through her strawberry-blonde curls, and she wore Mariella's clothes which were two sizes too big for her, while Mariella looked rather snug in Hannah's clothes!

🏃 🏃 🏃

Like most runners, I have a complicated relationship with Portaloos. I'm thrilled to see them before, during, and after a race, when I've consumed copious amounts of water and energy gels. But I can't say I've ever *enjoyed* being enclosed in one of these foul-smelling thunderboxes.

Needless to say, I was hesitant to introduce Mariella to a Portaloo for the first time. But as any parent with a toddler will tell you, when they say they need to go, you must get them to a toilet ASAP.

I used a single pinkie finger to open the door of the first cubicle, revealing a toilet seat and floor flooded in urine. I promptly let the door close shut. I was assaulted by a stomach-turning stack of turds in the toilet of the second cubicle. There was no way I was going to put my baby girl through an experience like that.

'Mummy, I have to go!' cried Mariella.

The situation was dire. John wouldn't have known to pack spare clothes in case of an emergency of this magnitude. The third cubicle I tried was the least offensive of the three — not that that's saying much!

'Okay, please don't touch anything,' I begged Mariella, stupidly forgetting that instructing a toddler to do something invariably leads to the opposite outcome.

CHAPTER 42

'The reason we race isn't so much to beat each
other…but to be with *each other.'*
—Christopher McDougall

BIG RED RUN
DAY 6

7 July 2014

It's all smiles in camp on the final morning of the Big Red Run. I swap my long compression pants for the pair of black adidas shorts I wore on the first two days. I can't wait to get back to the Birdsville Caravan Park and have a long, hot shower.

All that remains is an 'easy' eight-kilometre run, walk, crawl, or whatever else I can manage. Today's effort will be untimed, so even the competitive runners at the front of the pack can take a casual stroll into Birdsville without feeling pressure to maintain a speedy pace.

Geoff has written two notes for day six. I open the first one and read:

> *8km easy run — pfft. So it's the last day of racing*
> *aye? Well you've either made it this far or bombed out*
> *like a beginner on a six-foot wave — either way you're*

AWESOME! And if you're reading this early, you're a Cheekball.

Geoff knows I *hate* surprises, so I'm sure he expected me to have read all the notes before the race even started! It's rare for him to buy me a birthday or anniversary present without me finding out what it is in advance. I usually pretend that I'm super surprised and had no idea it was coming. I think we're both astounded that I've been able to resist opening his notes early.

We have a leisurely ten o'clock start. It feels like the slowest eight kilometres of my life! Yes, even slower than the final eight kilometres of the fifty-kilometre ultramarathon in Canberra. Every single millimetre of every single muscle hurts. I can't will my legs to run even if my life depended on it. I'm forced to take one small step at a time.

But knowing how close I am to the end helps me to keep pressing on. It takes me over an hour and ten minutes to reach the finish line at the Birdsville Hotel. This gives me plenty of time to soak it all in, and reflect on what I've accomplished over the last six days.

Spectators line the dusty street leading up to the Birdsville Hotel. I catch the melodic lilt of Welsh MC Adrian's voice, warmly welcoming the runners as they return to Birdsville. My smile is as big as Big Red as I hobble my way through the red inflatable archway.

I can't quite believe it; I've just run 150 kilometres through the Simpson Desert! My cumulative time for the event is one day, two hours, forty-six minutes, and fifty seconds, placing me in eighth position out of ten Little Red Runners — not that that matters!

'Well done, Steph!' exclaims a volunteer, reaching up to hang the finisher's medal around my neck.

I've never felt prouder to receive a medal than I am today. I don't think I'll ever forget the moment when the runners, volunteers, and supporters interlock their fingers to form a tunnel, cheering the final walkers over the finish line.

'I'm so proud of you, Steph,' says Dad, pulling me into a bear hug.

He doesn't need to say it; the tears glistening in his eyes give it away. Our adventure together began even before the race kicked off, and now here we are, back at the Birdsville Hotel. Dad and I have grown so much closer than I could have ever imagined possible before we set out on our epic outback road trip a couple of weeks ago.

I sit in the Birdsville Bakery, shovelling down one of their award-winning curried camel pies. Their website isn't lying when it says, 'It's a long way to the shop if you want a sausage roll, but it's worth the trip.'

I travelled almost two thousand kilometres in three days by car to reach Birdsville, and then covered 150 kilometres in six days on foot to complete the Big Red Run. I entered the Simpson Desert as one person, and will leave it as a completely different person.

The Big Red Run has become more than just a running race, or an opportunity to raise money to find a cure for type 1 diabetes. The incredible people I've met here started out as a bunch of strangers, but we've finished as lifelong friends after sharing the highs and lows of six crazy, wonderful days in the desert. Having pushed ourselves to the absolute limits of our physical and mental strength, we've forged some of the deepest friendships we'll probably ever experience in our lifetime.

I celebrate with my new friends at the Birdsville Hotel in the evening. I order a drink at the bar, and marvel at the old-world memorabilia on the walls. There are countless hats stuck to the ceiling, each one representing someone who spent more than a year in Birdsville doing the 'hard yards'.

I won't lie; I'm disappointed that I just did the 150-kilometre Little Red Run, rather than the full 250-kilometre Big Red Run. That word *just* often elicits playful jests from friends. Isn't it interesting how our perspective can vary so greatly from that of others?

As I slogged my way up Heartbreak Hill during my first City2Surf in 2009, there's no way I could have fathomed ever running further than fourteen kilometres, and I believed that anyone who willingly signed up for an ultramarathon was as mad as a hatter. But now *I'm* the insane one, wishing I'd run an extra one hundred kilometres!

I've never had dreams of becoming an elite athlete. Honestly, I don't even fit the image most people have of a runner — my feet turn inward like a penguin's, I have a slouched posture (a bully in primary school once called me 'Hunchback of Notre Dame'), I'm far from slim, and my knees are wonky. Gary's nickname for me is 'T-Rex' because he says my arm position when I run resembles a Tyrannosaurus Rex. I'm not exactly a graceful gazelle.

Then again, what is a runner *supposed* to look like? On day one of the Big Red Run, I couldn't help comparing myself to the other runners. I felt unworthy of wearing the same orange and blue race shirt as them, and questioned whether I had what it took to finish the race.

Turns out, I'd worried for nothing; the Big Red Run has taught me that ultrarunners come in all different shapes and sizes. I've proven to myself — and to others — that I'm just as capable of crossing the finish line as anyone else. I might be an everyday runner, but I'm more than okay with that.

🏃🏃🏃

I head back to the tent and crawl into my sleeping bag. I'm reflecting on one of the most challenging yet rewarding weeks of my life, when it crosses my mind that I still have Geoff's final note to read:

After day six of racing — finished!? If you've made it, CONGRATULATIONS! You're pretty much an ama-zeball. Wow! A-mazing! Fan-tastic! If you didn't quite make it, you're an awesomeball for trying so hard like I know you would have.

I can't wait to get back home to tell Geoff all about the Big Red Run. I want to tell him about both the good times and the bad. About the friend-ships I've made. About the life-changing lessons I've learned.

But first, sleep.

EPILOGUE

'Jesus spoke to them, saying, "I am the light of the world. Whoever follows me will not walk in darkness, but will have the light of life."'
—John 8:12

Why the dickens do I run long distances? This is a question that every ultrarunner asks themselves a million times. It's also a question that must be answered to keep us running. Clearly, it's not about the podium finish for me...

I run because I'm convinced that there's no better way to experience the sights, sounds, and smells of the world that God has generously created for us to enjoy.

I run because it keeps me healthy — both physically, by helping to manage my blood glucose levels, improve my cardiovascular fitness, and maintain my weight; and mentally, by boosting my self-esteem, and helping me deal with depression and anxiety.

I run because it's the perfect way to spend quality time with Geoff, enjoying each other's company as we explore new places and laugh at the funny things we come across.

I run because I want to be a healthy role model for my daughters, just like Mum was for me when she encouraged me to run my first City2Surf.

I run because I value being part of a supportive community of like-minded individuals who spur me on to do my best, regardless of how 'fast' or 'slow' I may be.

I run because I hope to inspire others, especially those living with type 1 diabetes, to never, ever let anything stop them from achieving their goals.

I run because I love to challenge myself. After every marathon, I tell myself, *Okay, that's enough long-distance running. I'll stick to shorter races now — no more than ten kilometres.* Yet a few months later, I find myself signing up for another marathon!

I run because *I can*!

James 1:12 says, 'Blessed is the one who perseveres under trial because, having stood the test, that person will receive the crown of life that the Lord has promised to those who love him' (NIV).

The Greek word translated here as *crown* is στέφανος, or *stephanos* (it's where the name 'Stephanie' comes from actually!). It refers to a garland, usually made of laurel leaves, given to the winners of running races at the ancient Olympic Games.

I'm sure the apostle Paul must have been a runner because he made so many references to the sport! In 1 Corinthians 9:24-26, Paul writes, 'Do you not know that in a race all the runners run, but only one gets the prize? Run in such a way as to get the prize. Everyone who competes in the games goes into strict training. They do it to get a crown that will not last, but we do it to get a crown that will last forever.'

Again, in Philippians 3:13b-14, Paul writes, 'One thing I do: forgetting what lies behind and straining forward to what lies ahead, I press on toward the goal to win the prize for which God has called me heavenward in Christ Jesus' (NIV).

I don't know how many kilometres I have left to run in this marathon of life. If I've learned anything over the years, it's that life is full of surprises. I might run a 250-kilometre race one day, or I might not. I might achieve my sub four-hour marathon goal someday, or I might not — and that's okay!

Just as my head torch died at the Big Red Run, forcing me to rely on others to navigate the path ahead, my faith journey has often felt like running in the dark, yet trusting that God is walking with me every step of the way. Even when I can't see the finish line, I can be confident that He will illuminate it in His perfect timing.

My prayer is that one day I'll stand before God, able to confidently declare, 'I have fought the good fight, I have finished the race, I have kept the faith' (2 Timothy 4:7). So I'll keep running with endurance the race that God has set before me, certain that the best is yet to come...

ACKNOWLEDGEMENTS

Writing this memoir has been a lot like running a marathon — a journey filled with satisfaction and excitement, as well as self-doubt and exhaustion. Getting it across the finish line demanded hours and hours of dedication, including writing, revising, and countless rounds of editing. Like any long-distance race, there were moments when I wanted to quit, and others when I hit the proverbial wall, uncertain how to press on.

I can hardly believe I'm finally here, a decade after writing my first word, celebrating the publication of my first book! This achievement wouldn't have been possible without the support of so many individuals who have stood by me through every stage of the process.

First and foremost, to God, whose strength has been my foundation throughout this creative journey. It was His calling that inspired me to write this story, which is ultimately *His* story, not mine. Thank you for constantly reminding me of my 'why'. My prayer is that *It's Not a Sprint* will bring You glory and make an eternal difference in the lives of all who read it.

To my wonderful husband, Geoff. This memoir would not exist without your unwavering love, support, and encouragement. Thank you for taking the girls out on all-day daddy-daughter dates while I poured my heart into these pages. Without you by my side, the kilometres I've covered — both in running and in life — would have been far less interesting. Cheekballs for life!

To my beautiful daughters, Mariella, Hannah, and Arna. Being your mum is the greatest joy and privilege of my life. I pray that God will guide me in passing on the baton of faith to each of you, and that you will cling to it as you run your own race. Remember to always keep your eyes on Jesus, no matter what obstacles you face along the way. I love you infinity.

To the world's best parents, David and Maria. Thank you for being there for me from the very beginning. You have taught me the importance of perseverance and hard work — qualities that have been essential not only for completing this project, but also for overcoming the challenges I've faced in my life. I love you so much, and I'm incredibly proud to be your daughter.

To my family and friends who have cheered me on, not only during this writing journey, but in my everyday life: Melissa, Chris, Daniel, Alicia, Aurelle, Marcelle, John, Leonora, Rob, Ben, Zara, Gary and many, many others. I'm sure you know who you are, and I hope you realise how much your support means to me! I'm blessed beyond measure to have you all in my life.

To my literary agent, Nicole Partridge. Thank you so much for believing in me and my writing. Your guidance and encouragement have been invaluable — from the first steps of editing to crossing the finish line of publication. I'll be forever grateful for your insightful manuscript assessment, and for all the effort you put into finding the perfect home for my memoir.

To the team at Ark House Press. Thank you for standing behind my story and bringing it to life in print. I have aspired to be a published author since I was a little girl, so I'm incredibly grateful for your partnership and expertise in making my dream a reality. Your guidance, assistance, and dedication to sharing my memoir with others mean the world to me.

To my beta readers: Geoff, Melissa, Aurelle, Mum, Dad, Seb, and Trudy. Thank you for investing your time into providing such thorough feedback. I'd like to especially acknowledge Mum and Melissa for their unmatched proofreading skills. I take full responsibility if there are typos in the final version — but please don't point them out or I might just die of shame.

To my Omega Writers friends. You have been a huge source of encouragement since I attended my first conference in 2022. I worried that I wouldn't fit in because I hadn't yet published a book, but you showed me that we're all running our own race, and God's timing is always perfect. Thank you for reminding me that the true purpose of our writing is to glorify God.

To my online writing group: Barbara, Dienece, Donna, Kel, Sue, and Suzie. Your commitment to showing up every Wednesday and Friday morning for our writing sprints is truly inspiring. Thank you for holding me accountable, motivating me to keep putting the words on the page, and teaching me so much about writing and the publishing industry.

To my Big Red Run friends. Whether we're cheering each other on at races or sharing the love with kudos on Strava, the camaraderie that still exists serves as a powerful reminder of our unforgettable week in the Simpson Desert. Ten years on, you continue to motivate me to do my best — not just in my running pursuits, but in everything I set out to achieve in life.

And finally, to the remarkably strong women in my life who share the burden of living with type 1 diabetes — Melissa, Amy, Anja, Claire, Emily, Igraine, Jenny, Lok, Monica, and Samar. Each and every one of you exemplifies true resilience and courage in the face of daily adversity. Never forget that even during the most challenging moments of your race, you are never running alone.

BEYOND THE FINISH LINE

Want exclusive access to a bonus chapter of *It's Not a Sprint?* Sign up on my website to discover the crazy adventures that follow the pages of this book.

From running a fifty-kilometre ultramarathon while pregnant with our third baby girl, to facing my fears and lining up for a hundred-metre parents' race at my daughter's school, and chasing that elusive sub-four-hour marathon time once again — this bonus chapter will inspire you with even more stories of faith and endurance!

Visit **www.stephaniewalters.com.au** to sign up today.

www.ingramcontent.com/pod-product-compliance
Lightning Source LLC
Chambersburg PA
CBHW030920090426
42737CB00007B/267